HOLIDAY CELEBRATIONS
Cookbook

COMPLETE MENUS & EASY RECIPES
FOR A FULL YEAR OF FESTIVITIES

SHADY OAK PRESS

Holiday Celebrations Cookbook

COMPLETE MENUS & EASY RECIPES
FOR A FULL YEAR OF FESTIVITIES

On Front Cover: Romantic and Relaxing Valentine's Gathering, page 28
On Page 1: A Patriotic 4th of July Menu, page 69

1 2 3 4 5 6 / 12 11 10 09 08 07
© 2002 North American Membership Group, Inc.
ISBN: 978-1-58159-346-4

Distributed by:
Sterling Publishing Co., Inc.
387 Park Avenue South
New York, NY 10016-8810

For information about custom editions, special sales, premium and corporate purchases, please contact Sterling Special Sales Department at 800-805-5489 or specialsales@sterlingpub.com.

Tom Carpenter
Creative Director

Julie Cisler
Book Design and Production

Macemon Photography
Commissioned Photographer

Kurt Adolfson
Assistant Photography

Susan Broscious
Food Stylist

Jerry Dudycha
Food Stylist Assistant

Michele Joy
Prop Stylist

Yula Nelson
Craft Stylist

Cort Sinnes
Craft Instruction and Artwork

SHADY OAK PRESS
12301 Whitewater Drive
Minnetonka, MN 55343

CONTENTS

INTRODUCTION

*Welcome to a full year's worth of
festive creations for holidays of all kinds!*

A year is filled with reasons to celebrate.

New Year's says goodbye to a wonderful year past and hello to new horizons. Valentine's Day brings a unique opportunity to tell someone you love how you really feel. Passover and Easter commemorate important religious events, and gather family together. The Fourth of July plays up patriotism and fun. Halloween lets holiday lovers of all ages make wholesome autumn revelry. Thanksgiving and Christmas cap off the year of celebrations with messages of good will and good cheer.

But besides the excitement they generate, these occasions all have something else significant in common: They are celebrated at events large to small, with family and/or friends … and often enough you are the host.

That's why we made the book you are holding and called it the *Holiday Celebrations Cookbook.* Here is a wonderful variety of festive creations you can use for holiday entertaining occasions of all kinds.

Now, you certainly have some of your own holiday traditions. But maybe you're looking for a few new ideas. Or a new way to celebrate. Or this year the event is at your house. Or you want to do something special for a holiday you've never observed before. No matter the reason, it's important to have an arsenal of holiday recipes and ideas at your fingertips!

To start, you get twenty complete menus, each consisting of a collection of great recipes designed to help you celebrate the event in style and with great food. Each occasion also includes a craft idea, complete with a list of materials you'll need and instructions on how to make it, so that you can further personalize, accessorize and beautify your celebrations.

Festivities are fun. Festivities are also important—for gathering together people who matter to you, and for sharing the plentiful bounties of good food, good friendship and good fun.

Make all your holiday celebrations special. The menus, ideas, insights and instructions are right here—all you add is a little love and care!

New Year's Eve Celebration

by Maria Lorraine Binchet

On the evening one year tumbles into the next, Champagne and festive foods are the tools of celebration. Champagne has traditionally been paired with expensive, elegant foods like caviar and smoked salmon, but it doesn't have to be. It works equally well with more casual foods like salted nuts, fried chicken and french fries! The reason? A basic Champagne and food pairing rule: effervescence loves fat and salt. By the way, it's the same reason soda pop works so well with potato chips or pretzels.

Champagne is known for its delicate apple, citrus and herbal flavors if it is Chardonnay-based (Blanc de Blancs) and for hints of berries if it is made from Pinot Noir (Blanc de Noirs). Subtle flavors of nuts, especially hazelnuts and almonds, are also quite common. In the recipes here, you will notice some flavors that pick up on those found in Champagne. See if the flavors of the food and Champagne melt seamlessly into one another when you taste the two together. Specific tasting notes accompany each recipe to guide you through the process. And remember, each person perceives flavors differently, so there are no right or wrong responses!

MENU

Easy Pâté and Wild Mushroom Ravioli

Caramelized Scallops with Fresh Fruit Salsa

Secret Fried Chicken Drumettes

CRAFT

Colorful Beaded Wine Glass Markers

EASY PÂTÉ AND WILD MUSHROOM RAVIOLI

Though you use only a small amount, wild mushrooms really make a difference in the flavor of this dish. And if you've never used hazelnut oil before, it is a fragrant, flavor-packed alternative to olive oil, excellent used in salad dressings and desserts. Here it adds a finishing touch to ravioli, as it does in the Champagne region of France.

½ **lb. pâté, smooth, creamy type, preferably duck or goose, at room temperature**
2 **oz. wild mushrooms, finely chopped**
2 **tablespoons chopped fresh chives**
1⅛ **teaspoon freshly ground pepper**
24 **wonton pasta wrappers (found in refrigerated produce section)**
Egg yolk mixed with ½ teaspoon water
4 **teaspoons hazelnut oil**

Champagne Tasting Notes
Hazelnut oil and the pâté's creaminess meet their match in the Champagne's bubbles and acidity. The nut flavor and fresh chives play into those same subtle Champagne flavors.

● In bowl, combine pâté, mushrooms, 1 tablespoon of the chives and pepper; set aside.

● In large pot, heat water for cooking ravioli.

● Put 6 of the wonton wrappers, with 1 corner of each at top, across cutting board. Place 1 scant teaspoon pâté filling in center of each wonton; brush top 2 sides with egg yolk wash. Fold bottom sides of wonton up over filling to meet top edges, forming a small triangle. Seal edges with fingers. Continue with remaining wrappers.

● Cook ravioli in batches, sliding them into gently simmering water, being sure not to crowd pot. Cook 3 to 4 minutes; remove carefully with slotted spoon to serving platter or individual plates. Immediately drizzle with hazelnut oil; garnish with remaining tablespoon chives.

● Alternative method: Make "beggar's purses" instead of ravioli by gathering all the edges of the wonton above filling to form "purse." Tie with chive to secure. Arrange in single layer in steamer coated with nonstick cooking spray; steam over a medium boil 8 minutes. Remove carefully.

8 appetizer portions.

Preparation time: 40 minutes.
Ready to serve: 40 minutes.

CARAMELIZED SCALLOPS WITH FRESH FRUIT SALSA

Fresh fruit salsas are a refreshing and highly flavorful accompaniment to fish. You can use any fruit in season, in any combination. Rather than buy an entire melon or pineapple, you can always buy a small piece of one.

SALSA
- **⅓ cup diced green apple**
- **⅓ cup diced green melon**
- **⅓ cup diced fresh pineapple**
- **3 tablespoons finely diced red onion**
- **2 tablespoons finely chopped fresh cilantro**
- **2 tablespoons lime juice**
- **1 teaspoon sugar**
- **½ teaspoon salt**

SCALLOPS
- **24 sea scallops (about 1¼-inch diameter), as fresh as possible**
- **1 teaspoon salt**
- **½ teaspoon freshly ground pepper**
- **1 teaspoon sugar**
- **4 teaspoons butter**

Champagne Tasting Notes
The fruit and herbal flavors of the salsa are similar to those in the wine. Scallops and Champagne share a similar delicacy or intensity; neither overpowers the other. The butteriness of the scallops is often matched by a similar and subtle butteriness in the Champagne.

● In bowl, combine apple, melon, pineapple, onion, cilantro, lime juice, 1 teaspoon sugar and ½ teaspoon salt. Adjust sweet-tart balance, if needed, by adding a bit more sugar or lime juice.

● Sprinkle each side of scallops with 1 teaspoon salt, pepper and 1 teaspoon sugar. In skillet, melt butter over medium-high heat. When butter barely begins to turn color, add scallops; cook 1½ to 2 minutes per side or until scallops are lightly browned. (Be careful not to crowd pan or overcook.) Arrange scallops on heated dish with *Fresh Fruit Salsa* in separate bowl, or place 3 scallops on each of 8 small serving plates with *Fresh Fruit Salsa* on the side.

8 appetizer portions.

Preparation time: 15 minutes.
Ready to serve: 15 minutes.

SECRET FRIED CHICKEN DRUMETTES

The secret to great fried chicken? Brine it! And not just in any brine—a buttermilk brine. Drumettes, if you're unfamiliar with them, are the "drumstick" part of the wing. Fry them in peanut oil and enjoy this updated old-fashioned favorite as one year sets and the next one dawns.

BRINE

- 3 **cups buttermilk**
- 2 **tablespoons plus 1 teaspoon sugar**
- 2 **tablespoons plus 1 teaspoon salt**

CHICKEN

- 32 **chicken drumettes**
- 3 **cups all-purpose flour**
- 2 **teaspoons freshly ground pepper**
- 2 **teaspoons paprika**
- ¾ **teaspoon cayenne pepper**
- ½ **teaspoon salt**
- 3 to 4 **cups peanut oil or other vegetable oil**

Champagne Tasting Notes

Notice how the bubbles and the acid of the Champagne cut right through the fat of the fried chicken? It's a classic strategy in food and Champagne pairing. There's also a delicious temperature contrast between the hot fried chicken and the very cold Champagne.

● For brine: Heat buttermilk to lukewarm; add sugar and salt. Stir until completely dissolved; let cool. Pour over drumettes in shallow, nonreactive dish; refrigerate 24 hours.

● In large plastic bag, combine flour, ground pepper, paprika, cayenne and salt. Remove drumettes from brine then discard brine; add to flour mixture 6 at a time. Shake bag to coat thoroughly.

● In wok or deep-fat fryer, heat oil over medium-high heat until very hot. (Chopstick should sizzle when placed in oil.) Add drumettes, cooking in batches so as not to crowd wok or fryer. Fry drumettes, turning once, until crispy and golden on both sides and no longer pink in the center, about 15 minutes. Drain on paper towels; transfer to pretty platter. Serve immediately.

32 drumettes.

Preparation time: 40 minutes.
Ready to serve: 40 minutes, plus 24 hours for brining.

NOTE Champagne goes so well with fried foods, consider making a batch of french fries too. Use store-bought frozen shoestring fries or make your own. Serve in parchment paper cones.

Colorful Beaded Wine Glass Markers

Here is an elegant, inexpensive and remarkably easy way for your guests to never lose track of which wine glass is theirs. Each colorful beaded marker travels up the stem of the glass, adding a festive note of color to the holidays while making each glass distinctive from the rest.

MATERIALS

For each beaded wine glass marker you will need:
- **one 7-inch length of .06 mm (22 gauge) or .08 mm (20 gauge) brass-covered copper wire**
- **2 tiny (about 3 mm) gold-colored beads**
- **2 small (about 4 mm) gold-colored beads**
- **Large colorful decorative bead (about 9 to 10 mm)**
- **2 medium beads (about 7 mm) in same color as large bead**
- **jewelry pliers or other fine-tipped needle-nose pliers**
- **jewelry wire cutter, or very sturdy scissors**

INSTRUCTIONS

1. To form loop at end of wire, place point of jewelry pliers at extreme tip of one end of wire. In one continuous movement, turn the pliers away from you in an extremely tight circle until tip of wire touches length of wire. Loop should be anywhere from ¹⁄₁₆ to ⅛ inch long.

2. Thread beads in this order: small gold, medium colored, large colored, small gold. Carefully bend wire at 45° angle to keep beads from moving down wire. Then thread beads onto wire in this order: tiny gold, medium colored, tiny gold. Make loop on other end of wire same as in the beginning. Move second group of beads down to new end loop, and bend wire as before to secure beads at this end.

3. To wrap marker around glass, hold end of wine glass marker with larger bead on base of wine glass where it meets the stem. While holding end in place, twist wire up and around stem.

4. Remove markers from wine glasses before washing but keep them in their "corkscrew" spiral shape. They'll be easier to put on the glasses next time!

Variations
Use more beads, different shapes of beads or different colors of wire. Combine two colors of beads but keep the combinations simple and distinct for easy identification.

A Very Adult New Year's Eve with Friends

by Melanie Barnard

Some people love the noisy horn blowers and revelry of the crowd, and some people (like me) prefer to welcome the New Year in the quiet company of a few special friends and family. This is a very adult New Year's Eve menu for four. If there are a few more very special people in your life, each recipe can easily be doubled or even tripled. If revelry is not your style, then save the menu, halve the recipes and make this elegant little supper à deux for Valentine's Day.

Whenever you choose to celebrate, this menu is ideal since much of the food can be made ahead of time, save the soufflé, which ought to be frothed up and baked in the company of friends anyway. The sauce for the game hens can be made a day ahead and the hens themselves assembled early in the day. The wild rice and broccoli are easily reheated and you can mix the salad vinaigrette several hours in advance. The soufflé is a miraculous dessert to prepare, share and savor with others.

MENU

Blood Orange Game Hens with Mustard Port Wine Sauce

Herbed Wild Rice and Cranberry Pilaf

Roasted Broccoli and Bell Peppers

Mâche Salad with Stilton and Walnuts

Chocolate Truffle Soufflés

CRAFT

Elegant Gift Boxes

Blood Orange Game Hens with MustardPort Wine Sauce

Blood oranges, so called because of their ruby red flesh and juice, have a distinctive tart flavor, but you can substitute the more readily available seedless naval oranges here. Game hens are wonderfully festive and make a pretty plate presentation for a sophisticated little supper. Ask the butcher to cut the hens in half, saving you the effort and giving you more time to set a holiday table.

2 blood oranges or naval oranges
2 large Cornish game hens (about 1½ lb. each), halved
2 teaspoons chopped fresh thyme
Salt and freshly ground pepper
¾ cup ruby Port
¼ cup currant jelly
1½ tablespoons Dijon mustard
1 tablespoon red wine vinegar
2 teaspoons Worcestershire sauce

● Heat oven to 450°F. Cut 4 thin slices from 1 of the oranges; cut each slice in half. Grate 2 teaspoons peel from remaining oranges, then squeeze ¼ cup juice; reserve peel and juice.

● Use your fingers to loosen skin of game hen halves. Insert 2 orange slice halves and ½ teaspoon thyme under skin of each hen half. Season hens with salt and pepper. Place, skin-side up, on rimmed baking sheet. Bake 15 minutes.

● Meanwhile, in medium saucepan, bring Port and jelly to a boil, stirring until jelly is melted and smooth. Simmer, uncovered, until lightly reduced, 4 to 5 minutes. Stir in Dijon, vinegar, Worcestershire, orange peel and orange juice. Simmer 2 minutes, stirring often.

● Brush hens with sauce. Continue baking, brushing once or twice with sauce, until meat is no longer pink, juices run clear and skin is richly browned, about 15 minutes.

● Boil sauce until just syrupy, about 2 minutes. Spoon sauce over hens to serve.

4 servings, with ½ cup sauce.

Preparation time: 30 minutes.
Ready to serve: 1 hour.

HERBED WILD RICE AND CRANBERRY PILAF

Wild rice is not really rice at all, but an aquatic grass native to North America, especially the northern plains. Its flavor is uniquely nutty and earthy, well suited to autumn meals. Depending upon the freshness of the raw rice, it will take varying amounts of time to cook. The best test of doneness is when individual grains begin to split apart.

2	tablespoons butter
1	medium onion, chopped (about 1 cup)
1	large rib celery, chopped (about ½ cup)
2½ to 3	cups reduced-sodium chicken broth
1	cup raw wild rice
2	tablespoons chopped fresh sage
½	teaspoon salt, plus more to taste
¼	teaspoon freshly ground pepper, plus more to taste
⅓	cup dried cranberries
1	tablespoon lemon juice

● In heavy 3-quart saucepan, melt butter; cook onion and celery over medium heat, stirring often, just until softened, about 3 minutes. Add 2½ cups broth, wild rice, 1 tablespoon of the sage, ½ teaspoon salt and ¼ teaspoon pepper. Bring to a boil; cover. Reduce heat to low; simmer gently until rice grains begin to split, about 50 minutes.

● Stir in cranberries; add more broth if rice seems dry. Cover; continue simmering until liquid is absorbed and rice grains are al dente, 10 to 15 minutes. Stir in lemon juice and remaining tablespoon sage; season with salt and pepper.

4 servings (4½ cups).

Preparation time: 20 minutes.
Ready to serve: 1 hour, 25 minutes.

ROASTED BROCCOLI AND BELL PEPPERS

Lots of vegetables roast beautifully, but none better than broccoli and bell peppers, whose colors and flavors intensify deeply during a brief sojourn in a hot oven with nothing more than olive oil and garlic. Roast the vegetables along with the hens, or cook them early in the day and simply reheat in the oven.

1 bunch broccoli (about 1 lb.), trimmed into florets with about 1½ inches stem
1 large red bell pepper, cut into 1½-inch-wide strips
1 large yellow bell pepper, cut into 1½-inch-wide strips
¼ cup olive oil
2 large garlic cloves, finely chopped
Salt and freshly ground pepper

● Heat oven to 450°F. Spread broccoli and bell peppers in single layer on large baking sheet. In small dish, combine oil and garlic. Brush vegetables on both sides with flavored oil. Bake, turning once, until vegetables are crisp-tender and lightly charred, 10 to 12 minutes. Season with salt and pepper.

● Serve vegetables warm or at room temperature. Vegetables can be roasted up to 4 hours in advance and kept at cool room temperature.

4 servings.

Preparation time: 15 minutes.
Ready to serve: 30 minutes.

MÂCHE SALAD WITH STILTON AND WALNUTS

For real sophistication, serve this salad European-style as a separate course after the main course. Or serve it American-style as a first course. Either way, it is elegant enough to stand on its own.

VINAIGRETTE

- ¼ **cup Champagne vinegar or white wine vinegar**
- 2 **teaspoons finely chopped shallot**
- 1 **teaspoon Dijon mustard**
- ½ **teaspoon salt**
- ¼ **teaspoon freshly ground pepper**
- ¼ **cup walnut oil**
- 2 **tablespoons mild olive oil**

SALAD

- 10 **cups mâche or other tender lettuce mixture**
- ¼ **cup walnut pieces, toasted**
- 4 **oz. Stilton cheese, cut into 4 wedges**

● For Vinaigrette: In bowl, whisk together vinegar, shallot, Dijon, salt and pepper. Whisk in walnut and olive oils.

● For Salad: Toss mâche with ⅓ cup of the vinaigrette; divide among 4 salad plates. Sprinkle with walnuts; place 1 cheese wedge on each salad. Serve with remaining vinaigrette.

4 servings.

Preparation time: 15 minutes.
Ready to serve: 15 minutes.

CHOCOLATE TRUFFLE SOUFFLÉS

These soufflés need to be assembled shortly before serving, but take only a few minutes' work and are a labor of love for such an impressive result. For New Year's Eve, you might want to wait until just before midnight to put them together. Then serve this ultimate chocolate experience with a glass of Champagne as the clock strikes midnight.

Butter and sugar, for soufflé dishes
4 chocolate truffles, each about 1 inch in diameter*
2 eggs, separated, plus 2 egg whites, at room temperature
½ cup sugar
¼ cup unsweetened cocoa, preferably European-style
1 tablespoon Kahlúa or coffee-flavored syrup
1 teaspoon vanilla
¼ teaspoon cream of tartar
Unsweetened whipped cream or vanilla ice cream (optional)

● Heat oven to 375°F. Generously butter 4 (8-oz.) soufflé dishes, deep ramekins or custard cups. Coat each with sugar, shaking out excess. Place 1 truffle in bottom of each dish.

● In small mixing bowl, beat egg yolks and 2 tablespoons sugar with mixer at high speed until lightened in color, 2 to 3 minutes. Beat in cocoa, Kahlúa and vanilla at low speed.

● In large mixing bowl, beat 4 egg whites until frothy. Beat in cream of tartar until soft peaks form. Gradually beat in remaining 6 tablespoons sugar until whites are glossy and stiff, but not dry. Stir ½ cup whites into cocoa mixture; fold remaining cocoa mixture into beaten whites. Divide soufflé mixture among dishes; place on baking sheet.

● Bake until soufflés are well risen and appear set on top, 17 to 19 minutes. Serve immediately with whipped cream or ice cream.

TIP *Though chocolate truffles are luxurious, you might try using bite-size Reese's Peanut Butter Cups®, Snickers® or Hershey's Kisses®, instead. Or, set out an assortment and let your guests choose their own soufflé centers!

4 soufflés.

Preparation time: 20 minutes.
Ready to serve: 40 minutes.

legant Gift Boxes

There's something almost magical about small boxes, elegantly wrapped. Shown here are plain gift boxes, the tops and bottoms of which have been wrapped separately in sophisticated wrapping paper. Complementary tissue paper lines the inside of the boxes, which can be filled with anything from an engagement ring to a chocolate "kiss" to lovely little party favors. Start the New Year right by placing one gift box atop each dinner plate to let your guest (or guests) know how special they are to you! Add a name tag and these pretty boxes can double as place cards.

MATERIALS

- **Small gift boxes with separate lids (available at craft stores)**
- **Fancy wrapping paper**
- **Spray adhesive or craft glue**
- **X-acto knife**
- **Tissue paper**
- **Party favors such as lottery tickets, noisemakers, paper crowns, plastic trinkets ... use your imagination, have fun**
- **Metallic gold cord or ribbon**

INSTRUCTIONS

1. Cut the wrapping paper for both the top and the bottom of the box, making sure it is large enough to go both up the outside edge of the box or lid as well as the inside edges.

2. Spray or apply glue to the inside of the pre-cut wrapping paper. Place the box in the center of the paper. Using the X-acto knife, cut wedge shapes from each corner, as shown in the illustration above.

3. Fold the paper up the sides of the box, pressing firmly in place, and then down the inside edges.

4. Cut the tissue paper so it fits neatly inside the box.

5. Fill the box with the party favors of your choice.

6. Tie the box with ribbon. Add a name tag if desired.

"Home for the Holidays" New Year's Day

by Carole Brown

Start the new year with family and friends and lots of good food. Baskets of munchable Lemon-Dill Pita Crisps *will disappear in no time. Your guests will warm up to the great flavors of bubbling* Hot Cheese Sandwiches with Sausage, Apples and Onions. *From a buffet, they can help themselves to* Fruit Salad with Raspberry Sauce and Ricotta Cheese, *and mugs of* Hearty Minestrone. *For a big finish, gather around the pot for* Mint Chocolate Fondue *and lots of dunking fun.*

MENU

Lemon-Dill Pita Crisps

Fruit Salad with Raspberry Sauce and Ricotta Cheese

Hearty Minestrone

Hot Cheese Sandwiches with Sausage, Apples and Onions

Mint Chocolate Fondue

CRAFT

Surprise-Filled Balloons

LEMON-DILL PITA CRISPS

Turn pita bread into delicious snack chips to nibble on while playing holiday games. Serve these chips solo or with a favorite sour cream, yogurt or hummus dip. They are also good with soups or salads. You can make the lemon-dill seasoning in advance. This recipe works best with thin pita bread that separates easily into pockets. If your pita bread does not pull apart, you'll need six rounds instead of three to make the same number of crisps. The thicker bread will be less crisp after baking, but still delicious.

6	tablespoons extra-virgin olive oil
1	garlic clove, pressed or finely minced
2	teaspoons dried dill weed
	Finely minced peel of 1 lemon*
¼	teaspoon salt
	Generous amount freshly ground pepper
	Dash cayenne pepper
3	pita pocket bread rounds or 6 solid pita bread rounds
1 to 2	tablespoons fennel seeds, sesame seeds, cumin seeds or dill seeds

TIP *If necessary, substitute 1 tablespoon good-quality dried lemon peel.

72 crisps.

Preparation time: 10 minutes.
Ready to serve: 30 minutes.

VARIATION To make a tasty party dip, stir lemon-dill mixture (about 6 tablespoons) into 2 cups plain yogurt. Add more salt and pepper to taste. Serve with unbaked pita wedges, raw vegetables and olives.

● Heat oven to 300°F. In bowl, mix oil, garlic, dill weed, lemon peel, salt, pepper and cayenne. Taste; adjust seasoning (mixture should be highly seasoned).

● Cut each pita into 12 wedges. Pull each wedge apart into 2 pieces to make 24 chips per round. (For solid pita that won't pull apart, cut 6 rounds into 12 wedges each.)

● Scoop ⅛ to ¼ teaspoon dill mixture onto each wedge; spread evenly. Stir dill mixture frequently as you scoop to keep ingredients evenly distributed. Lay wedges on baking sheet; sprinkle with seeds.

● Bake 15 to 20 minutes or until wedges are crisp and lightly browned. Watch crisps closely after 10 minutes of baking; they brown quickly during the last minutes.

FRUIT SALAD WITH RASPBERRY SAUCE AND RICOTTA CHEESE

This colorful salad will star at your party table. You can make the raspberry sauce and slice the melons a few hours ahead, but wait to slice the kiwi fruit until you are ready to serve. Ask your produce department for the most flavorful winter melons in your area.

RASPBERRY SAUCE

1	(15-oz.) can peach slices in light syrup
1	(14- or 16-oz.) bag frozen unsweetened raspberries, thawed
¼	teaspoon ground ginger
	Dash salt
2	tablespoons balsamic vinegar

SALAD

1	orange-fleshed winter melon, peeled, seeded
3 to 4	kiwi fruit
2	cups ricotta cheese*
1	cup raspberries, for garnish
½	cup finely chopped pistachios, for garnish

● Scoop peaches from syrup; place in food processor. Add 2 tablespoons syrup; blend until smooth, adding more syrup if necessary.

● In food processor bowl, blend raspberries with their juice until smooth; strain. Stir ½ cup peach puree into strained raspberries (reserve remaining puree for another use); add ginger, salt and balsamic vinegar.

● Slice melon into 24 thin crescents. Trim ends from kiwi fruit; stand on end and peel down sides with paring knife. Cut in half lengthwise; remove core from each side with shallow V-cut. Cut each half into 6 slices.

● Put 2 tablespoons raspberry sauce on each plate; arrange 4 melon and kiwi slices on top. Add dollop ricotta. Garnish with raspberries; dust with pistachios.

● Arrange fruit on platter; dust with pistachios. Serve raspberry sauce and ricotta on the side.

TIP *Substitute a smaller amount of a higher-fat cream such as sour cream, mascarpone or Devon cream if you wish.

8 to 10 servings.

Preparation time: 40 minutes.
Ready to serve: 40 minutes.

HEARTY MINESTRONE

Expect your friends to ask for the recipe after tasting this soup. Don't be alarmed by the long ingredient list—most are seasonings. Some canned and frozen vegetables are used to minimize prep time. It's a thick soup with lots of vegetables; you can add more broth if you wish. This soup is especially good the day after it's made.

3 tablespoons extra-virgin olive oil
1½ cups diced onions
¾ cup diced carrots
¾ cup diced celery
¼ cup packed shredded fresh basil
¼ cup packed chopped fresh parsley, preferably Italian parsley
1½ tablespoons fresh rosemary or 2 teaspoons dried
2 teaspoons dried thyme
⅛ teaspoon crushed red pepper
3 garlic cloves, minced
½ teaspoon salt
1 (28-oz.) can whole tomatoes, crushed, undrained
2 bay leaves
8 cups reduced-sodium chicken, beef or vegetable broth
1½ cups frozen cut or Italian green beans
3 medium zucchini, diced (about 1½ cups)
3 oz. small pasta shells (¾ cup)
1 (15-oz.) can cannellini or Great Northern beans, drained, rinsed
Salt and freshly ground pepper to taste
2 tablespoons shredded fresh basil and/or parsley, for garnish
1 cup freshly grated Parmesan cheese, for garnish

● Heat soup pot or Dutch oven over medium heat; add oil, onions, carrots, celery, ¼ cup basil, ¼ cup parsley, rosemary, thyme and crushed red pepper. Cook 5 minutes, stirring occasionally, or until vegetables start to soften. Add garlic, salt, tomatoes, bay leaves and broth. Simmer 15 minutes or until vegetables are almost soft. Add green beans and zucchini; simmer 20 minutes. (Soup can be prepared to this point, cooled and refrigerated overnight. The next day, reheat and continue with recipe.)

● In separate pan, cook pasta in salted water until al dente; drain. Add to soup along with cannellini beans. Taste; adjust seasoning. Simmer until all ingredients are hot. Stir in 2 tablespoons fresh basil and/or parsley and Parmesan just before serving.

6 to 8 servings (12½ cups).

Preparation time: 1 hour.
Ready to serve: 1 hour.

HOT CHEESE SANDWICHES WITH SAUSAGE, APPLES AND ONIONS

Both kids and adults will really dig into this fun party food. Make the cheese mixture in advance. Choose your favorite precooked sausage, such as frankfurters, Polish sausage, kielbasa, bologna, andouille or ham. Rye and pumpernickel breads are especially good here.

CHEESE

- 2 lb. sharp cheddar or other full-flavored cheese, grated (2 packed cups)
- 2 teaspoons Dijon or prepared mustard
- 1 teaspoon Worcestershire sauce Dash each of salt, freshly ground pepper and cayenne pepper
- 3 tablespoons beer, nonalcoholic beer or milk

SANDWICHES

- 2 tablespoons canola or other vegetable oil
- 2 medium onions, diced (about 2 cups)
- 1 lb. cooked sausage, cut into bite-size chunks
- 2 apples, peeled, cored and cut into bite-size chunks
- 2 teaspoons salt Freshly ground pepper to taste
- 8 to 10 slices hearty bread, toasted, if desired

● In bowl, mix cheese, mustard, Worcestershire, dash salt, pepper, cayenne and beer with spoon or your hands to thoroughly moisten cheese and distribute seasonings evenly.

● Place oven rack at least 3 inches from broiler.

● In heavy skillet, heat oil over medium-high heat. Add onions; toss. Reduce heat to medium. Cover; cook, stirring occasionally, 3 to 5 minutes or until onions are golden brown and soft. Add sausage, apples, 2 teaspoons salt and pepper; sauté 5 minutes or until apples are cooked but not mushy.

● Place bread on baking sheet; divide sausage mixture evenly among slices. Pat about 2 tablespoons cheese mixture on each sandwich. Broil until cheese is bubbly and lightly toasted. Serve immediately. Pass with additional mustard, if desired.

8 to 10 sandwiches.

Preparation time: 25 minutes.
Ready to serve: 30 minutes.

MINT CHOCOLATE FONDUE

This is the ultimate make-your-own dessert—a classic that never grows old. Choose the best-quality chocolate you can find (not chips). You can chop the chocolate well in advance (a strong serrated bread knife works well), but make the fondue itself just before serving. A food-warming or votive candle is enough to keep the chocolate soft.

SAUCE

 1½ **cups whipping cream**
 ¼ **cup light corn syrup**
  Dash salt
 1 **lb. bittersweet chocolate, chopped into small pieces**
¼ to ½ **teaspoon mint extract***

DUNKER IDEAS

 Cubes of angel food cake, pound cake, ladyfingers or fruit cake
 Biscotti, broken into bite-size chunks
 Tangerine segments
 Strawberries, whole or halved
 Cherries, whole or halved, pits removed
 Thick banana slices
 Dried or candied apricots
 Fresh or canned pineapple slices (pat dry with paper towel)
 Candied pineapple slices
 Star fruit (if ridges are too brown, trim with vegetable peeler before slicing into ¼-inch stars)
 Marshmallows
 Bowls of chopped nuts, flaked coconut or sprinkles, for dipping coated dunkers

● In small saucepan, bring cream, corn syrup and salt to a low boil.

● Place chocolate in bowl; pour warm cream mixture over chocolate. Let sit about 3 minutes to melt. Gently whisk until smooth; stir in mint extract.

● Put sauce in heatproof bowl or ceramic fondue pan; hold over food-warming candle. Spear dunkers with 6- or 8-inch bamboo skewers or long fondue forks for dipping.

TIPS *Alternatively, use any extract of your choice, such as cinnamon, coconut, coffee or orange. You can also substitute 2 teaspoons vanilla.

8 to 12 servings, about 3 cups sauce.

Preparation time: 40 minutes.
Ready to serve: 45 minutes.

VARIATION For an "adults only" fondue, substitute 2 to 4 tablespoons Grand Marnier, dark rum, Kahlúa, brandy or other liqueur for the extract. You can divide the fondue, making half of it nonalcoholic.

NOTE If you are lucky enough to have leftover sauce, use to top ice cream.

Surprise-Filled Balloons

If you're in the mood for a little raucous fun on New Year's Eve, these surprise-filled balloons are just the ticket, sure to please young and old alike. You'll need two helpers to assist in filling the balloons with rolled-up lottery tickets, confetti, party favors and the like. Once they are filled with goodies and air, write each guest's name on the side and use the balloon as a place card. Have some push pins on hand and pop balloons either at the beginning of the meal or, if you can wait, at the stroke of midnight.

MATERIALS

- **Large balloons**
- **Lottery tickets**
- **Small trinkets and goodies of every and any description**
- **Confetti**
- **Marking pen**

INSTRUCTIONS

1. Gather your helpers and give one person two chopsticks and the other person one chopstick.

2. Have your helpers put the chopsticks into the neck of the balloon and stretch the opening until it is wide enough to fill with the party favors of your choice. (Note: if you're including lottery tickets, you'll need to roll them first).

3. Inflate the balloons, tie off and, using a marking pen, write your guests' names on the outside.

Romantic and Relaxing Valentine's Gathering

by Michele Anna Jordan

Dim lights and candles enhance any meal, directing one's attention to the center of the table and the guests, who are flattered by the golden glow of surrounding candle flames. This atmosphere, while pleasing any time, is essential on Valentine's Day, so don't forget the candles and be sure to turn off any lights that may distract. This menu is designed to be enjoyed slowly and leisurely; much of it can be eaten without silverware, enhancing its sensual enjoyment. Spear scallops with a toothpick, pick up asparagus spears with your fingers ... and when you get to the chocolate truffles, you might consider feeding each other. As far as beverages go, dry Champagne works beautifully with each course.

MENU

Bay Scallop Martini

Warm Asparagus Vinaigrette with Prosciutto and Capers

Classic Cheese Fondue with Truffles, Baguettes and Fingerling Potatoes

Chilled Strawberry Soup

Chocolate Truffles with Cassis

CRAFT

Romantic Gold-Leafed Clam Shells

BAY SCALLOP MARTINI

When foods are marinated in acid for several hours, their protein denatures, which is exactly what happens when foods are heated, though then the process occurs more quickly. Thus, these scallops are not raw; rather, they are cooked using a different and gentler process.

½ lb. bay scallops, rinsed, drained, cooked
2 teaspoons kosher (coarse) salt, plus more as needed
½ cup plus 1 tablespoon fresh lime juice
¼ cup gin or vodka
2 tablespoons minced green olives
3 tablespoons olive oil
¼ teaspoon pimente d'esplette* or cayenne pepper
Salt and freshly ground pepper
4 martini olives on toothpicks

● In medium nonreactive container, toss scallops with 2 teaspoons salt. Pour ½ cup of the lime juice over scallops, tossing gently. Cover scallops; refrigerate, stirring occasionally, until scallops turn opaque, 4 to 6 hours.

● To serve, put 1 tablespoon of gin in 1 martini glass; swirl and pour it into second glass. Continue until each of the 4 glasses has been swirled with gin. Discard what remains of the gin; put glasses in freezer.

● In medium bowl, combine minced olives, oil, pimente d'esplette, remaining 3 tablespoons gin and remaining tablespoon lime juice. Taste; season with salt and pepper.

● Drain scallops, discarding liquid. Add scallops to bowl with dressing, tossing gently.

● Remove glasses from freezer (hold them by their stems so you don't fingerprint the bowls); quickly divide scallops among them. Garnish each with martini olive; serve immediately.

TIP *Pimente d'esplette is a mild ground chile from Basque country. Look for it under the "Igo" brand. Cayenne pepper is a good substitute.

4 servings (1½ cups).

Preparation time: 15 minutes.
Ready to serve: 6 hours, 15 minutes.

WARM ASPARAGUS VINAIGRETTE WITH PROSCIUTTO AND CAPERS

When you roast asparagus, a technique that intensifies its flavor, the spears need not be peeled.

1 lb. asparagus, tough stems snapped off
1 tablespoon olive oil
  Kosher (coarse) salt
  Freshly ground pepper
1 tablespoon Champagne vinegar
1½ teaspoons fresh lemon juice
1 small garlic clove, crushed, minced
1½ teaspoons minced fresh Italian parsley
¼ cup plus 1½ teaspoons extra-virgin olive oil
2 tablespoons capers, rinsed, drained
6 thin slices prosciutto, cut into ¼-inch-wide crosswise strips

● Heat oven to 475°F. Place asparagus on baking sheet; drizzle with 1 tablespoon oil. Toss lightly with your fingers until spears are coated. Season with salt and pepper; bake until asparagus is just tender, 8 to 12 minutes. Transfer to wide bowl; cover with tea towel.

● Meanwhile, in small bowl, mix vinegar, lemon juice, garlic and parsley. Season with salt and pepper; whisk in all but 1 tablespoon of the extra-virgin olive oil. Taste; adjust seasoning. In very small sauté pan, heat remaining tablespoon extra-virgin olive oil over medium-low heat; add capers. Fry, tossing frequently, until they swell and begin to open. Transfer immediately to small bowl.

● Pour vinaigrette over asparagus, tossing gently. Scatter with prosciutto; toss again. Divide asparagus mixture among individual serving plates; garnish each with capers.

4 servings.

Preparation time: 10 minutes.
Ready to serve: 20 minutes.

CLASSIC CHEESE FONDUE WITH TRUFFLES, BAGUETTES AND FINGERLING POTATOES

You will need a fondue pot, or something similar, to make this dish.

1½ lb. small fingerling potatoes, scrubbed, rinsed
1 to 2 tablespoons olive oil
Kosher (coarse) salt
Freshly ground pepper
1 large garlic clove, cut in half lengthwise
¾ lb. Gruyère cheese, cut into cubes
¾ lb. Emmenthaler cheese, cut into cubes
3 oz. taleggio cheese
¾ cup dry white wine
Freshly ground white pepper
2 tablespoons Cognac
2 tablespoons white truffle oil
1 black or white truffle*, thinly shaved (optional)
1 small bunch Italian parsley
2 fresh sourdough baguettes, torn into 1½-inch pieces

● Heat oven to 375°F. Cut potatoes in half lengthwise; place in saucepan. Cover with water; bring to a boil. Reduce heat; simmer 8 minutes or until potatoes are almost tender. Drain; put potatoes on baking sheet. Drizzle oil on potatoes; season with salt and black pepper. Bake, turning occasionally, until completely tender, about 15 minutes.

● Rub inside of fondue pot with garlic; discard garlic. Put cheeses and wine into pot; set over medium-low heat until cheeses are just melted. Stir with wooden spoon until mixture is thick and creamy. Season with white pepper; stir in Cognac and truffle oil. Sprinkle fondue with shaved truffle, if using.

● Spread parsley over platter; pile potatoes in center. Surround with baguette pieces; serve immediately alongside fondue. Use long-handled heatproof forks or long bamboo skewers to dip pieces of bread and potato in fondue.

TIP *Truffles, the tasty fungus that grows underground, are readily available on several web sites. Use your search engine to discover active truffle marketers. Truffles are expensive, but you need just a few grams to add tremendous flavor.

4 servings.

Preparation time: 25 minutes.
Ready to serve: 40 minutes.

CHILLED STRAWBERRY SOUP

If you've never had soup for dessert, you will be surprised at how satisfying and refreshing it is. You'll be delighted by this creation's sweet, fragrant flavors ... yet you won't feel too full.

3 pints (about 2¾ lb.) strawberries, stems removed, diced
¼ to ½ cup sugar to taste, plus more as needed
Dash ground cardamom (optional)
2 cups white wine, such as sauvignon blanc or dry rosé, plus more for thinning
Freshly ground pepper
2 tablespoons fresh mint, thinly sliced

● Put strawberries into large bowl; sprinkle with sugar. Cover; refrigerate 2 hours.

● Remove strawberries from refrigerator; stir. Remove 2 cups strawberries; set aside. If using, add cardamom to remaining strawberries; stir in 2 cups wine. Puree with immersion blender until mixture is smooth. (If you do not have an immersion blender, puree in standard blender or food processor; do not overmix.) Stir in reserved 2 cups strawberries.

● Taste for flavor and texture. If soup seems bland, stir in more sugar, 2 teaspoons at a time, until flavors blossom. If soup is too thick, stir in a bit more wine to achieve proper consistency. Season with pepper; stir. Cover; refrigerate until soup is chilled through, about 2 hours.

● To serve, ladle soup into wide soup plates; season with pepper. Garnish with mint.

4 servings (6½ cups).

Preparation time: 25 minutes.
Ready to serve: 4 hours, 25 minutes.

CHOCOLATE TRUFFLES WITH CASSIS

It is best to form these sweet, handmade truffles in a cool room. If your kitchen is particularly warm during the day, turn down the heat for a couple of hours, make truffles on a porch or patio, or consider making them at night.

½ **lb. bittersweet chocolate, preferably Scharffen Berger, broken into pieces**
3 **tablespoons cassis (black currant liqueur)**
5 **pasteurized egg yolks**
  Dash kosher (coarse) salt
½ **cup unsalted butter, cut into pieces, at room temperature**
1½ **cups powdered sugar, sifted**
¼ **cup unsweetened cocoa**

● Pour water into bottom of double boiler to about one-third full; water should not touch bottom of insert. Bring to a boil over high heat; reduce heat to low so water just barely simmers. Put chocolate and cassis in insert; set insert on top of simmering water, letting chocolate slowly melt. When fully melted, transfer insert to work surface; gently whisk in egg yolks, one at a time. Add salt and butter, a piece at a time, mixing well after each addition. Add about one-third of the powdered sugar; beat well. Add the next third; beat again. Add remaining sugar. When all of the sugar has been incorporated and mixture is smooth and velvety, refrigerate it, covered, until chilled through.

● To form truffles, remove chilled dough from refrigerator; place cocoa in medium mixing bowl. Coat palms of your hands with a little of the cocoa; place about 1½ teaspoons of the truffle mixture in palm of 1 hand. Roll between palms until it forms a ball; drop it into bowl of cocoa, shaking bowl to fully coat truffle. Set truffle on tray. When all of the truffles have been rolled, cover and refrigerate until ready to serve.

About 3 dozen truffles.

Preparation time: 40 minutes.
Ready to serve: 2 hours, 40 minutes.

ℛomantic Gold-Leafed Clam Shells

*O*kay, we know: Pearls grow inside of *oysters—not clams—but it's Valentine's Day and you'll be forgiven for using a little poetic license. Not unlike finding a message in a bottle, these gold-leafed clam shells can hold any surprise you like, from jewelry to real gold. We filled ours with an assortment of "pearls" and a rolled-up love note. You'll be happy as a clam after this Valentine's Day celebration.*

INSTRUCTIONS

1. Pick out the largest clams you can find. Add an inch or so of water in a small pan and bring to a boil. Drop clams into the water and cover; clams will open in a few minutes' time. Remove from water and allow to cool. Clean and wash the clam shells and allow to completely dry.

2. Paint adhesive on the outside of clam shells, according to the instructions included with the gold leaf kit. Allow to dry.

 3. Cut sections of gold leaf large enough to fit over clam shell, from side to side. Press gold leaf firmly into place, using your thumbs. Peel backing off to reveal a gold-leafed shell. Continue process until both top and bottom of shell have been completely covered with gold leaf.

4. Fill clam shells with party presents of your choice (note: if you decide to include a love note, cut a small strip of paper—small enough in width to fit inside the shell—and roll up like a scroll and tie tightly with the curling ribbon).

5. Use the fine brass wire as you would ribbon to hold both sides of the clam shell together.

MATERIALS

- **Large clam shells, cleaned and dried**
- **Gold leaf and gold leaf adhesive (available at craft stores)**
- **Imitation pearls**
- **Writing paper**
- **Curling ribbon**
- **Fine brass wire**

Be My Valentine Dinner for Two

by Mary Evans

Because the way to anyone's heart is often through the stomach, this menu is sure to win kudos if not undying affection. Make most of the menu earlier in the day. Start with the tarts; cover loosely with plastic wrap and store on the kitchen counter. Put the caramel sauce together and refrigerate, covered, until ready to reheat. Make the vinaigrette and refrigerate until you're ready to toss the salad. Roast the leeks ahead and have the spinach leaves ready for tossing. The Parmesan crisps and filling are also do-aheads; store the filling in the refrigerator, covered, until just before serving. You can even precook the vegetables and store them, covered, also in the refrigerator. Just microwave until heated through when it's time to eat. Broil the skewers and make the fondue sauce before serving and you'll have time to enjoy the meal—and each other.

MENU

Parmesan Crisps with Roasted Pepper Tapenade

Spinach and Roasted Leek Salad with Champagne Vinaigrette

Beef Skewers with Winter Vegetables and Cambozola Fondue Sauce

Walnut, Sage and Onion Breadstick Twists

Individual Heart-Shaped Pear Tarts with Caramel Sauce

CRAFT

Valentine Champagne Bucket

PARMESAN CRISPS WITH ROASTED PEPPER TAPENADE

Tapenade is a French, olive-based spread, that here also includes marinated artichokes and roasted bell peppers. To save time, buy bell peppers already roasted in a jar at your supermarket. Keep them on hand in your refrigerator to use in salads and sandwiches.

CRISPS
½ cup shredded Parmesan cheese

TAPENADE
3 tablespoons chopped, well-drained, marinated artichoke hearts
2 tablespoons chopped pitted imported black olives, such as Kalamata
1 tablespoon chopped roasted red bell pepper
   Dash dried thyme

● Heat oven to 375°F. Place Parmesan in 6 mounds on parchment-lined baking sheet. Press into 2-inch circles. Bake 4 to 6 minutes or until melted and golden. Let rest 2 to 3 minutes or until crisps are still flexible but firm enough to lift with spatula. Place over inverted mini-muffin cups, pressing gently to drape slightly. Let cool; remove. Invert to form cups.

● Meanwhile, in small bowl, combine artichoke hearts, olives, roasted bell pepper and thyme. Divide mixture evenly among *Parmesan Crisps.*

2 (3-crisp) servings.

Preparation time: 20 minutes.
Ready to serve: 20 minutes.

SPINACH AND ROASTED LEEK SALAD WITH CHAMPAGNE VINAIGRETTE

The roasted leeks become brown and crunchy, contrasting nicely with the torn spinach leaves.

CHAMPAGNE VINAIGRETTE
- **1 teaspoon Dijon mustard**
- **1 tablespoon Champagne vinegar**
- **⅛ teaspoon salt**
  Dash freshly ground pepper
- **2 tablespoons canola oil**

SALAD
- **1 small leek**
- **1 teaspoon canola oil**
- **2 cups torn spinach leaves, stems removed**

● In small bowl, whisk together mustard, Champagne vinegar, salt and pepper; whisk in 2 tablespoons oil.

● Heat oven to 425°F. Trim leek, removing root end and using white and pale green part only; cut in half lengthwise. Cut in ½-inch-wide strips. Toss with 1 teaspoon oil in shallow baking pan; spread in single layer. Bake 12 to 15 minutes, stirring once, or until most of leek strips are well browned. Remove; let cool. To serve, in large bowl, toss spinach with vinaigrette until coated. Divide between 2 chilled salad plates; top with leeks.

2 servings.

Preparation time: 30 minutes.
Ready to serve: 30 minutes.

BEEF SKEWERS WITH WINTER VEGETABLES AND CAMBOZOLA FONDUE SAUCE

Cambozola is a German cheese that combines the flavors of Camembert and Gorgonzola. For a heartier blue cheese flavor, use regular Gorgonzola. Serve this hearty dish with an Italian Chianti or French Côtes du Rhône wine.

WINTER VEGETABLES
- **2 (3-inch) red boiling potatoes, quartered**
- **1 medium carrot, cut in 1-inch pieces**
- **¾ cup cauliflower florets**

CAMBOZOLA FONDUE SAUCE
- **1 tablespoon butter**
- **1 tablespoon all-purpose flour**
- **¾ cup milk**
- **4 oz. diced Cambozola cheese, rind removed (or Gorgonzola or blue cheese)**
- **⅔ cup shredded mozzarella cheese**
- **1 tablespoon dry Marsala**

BEEF SKEWERS
- **2 (6- to 8-oz.) beef tenderloin steaks, cut in quarters**
- **4 wooden skewers, soaked in water 30 minutes**

● In medium saucepan, boil potatoes in salted water over medium-high heat. Add carrot; reduce heat to medium. Add cauliflower after 6 minutes; continue cooking 6 to 9 minutes or until tender. Drain; place in microwave-safe serving bowl. Cover to retain heat.

● In small saucepan, melt butter over medium-low heat; whisk in flour. Stir frequently, 1 to 2 minutes. Slowly whisk in milk; bring to a boil, whisking constantly. Boil 1 minute. Reduce heat to low; whisk in Cambozola and mozzarella until melted. Stir in Marsala. Place in small heatproof bowl over glass warmer.

● Meanwhile, heat broiler. Thread 2 pieces beef, slightly separated, on each skewer. Broil 4 to 6 inches from heat for 4 minutes. Turn and broil 3 to 6 minutes more.

● To serve, microwave vegetables 1 to 2 minutes or until piping hot. Place 2 skewers on each plate. Serve with vegetables, fondue sauce and fondue forks. Dip beef and vegetables in sauce. Serve with *Walnut, Sage and Onion Breadstick Twists* for dipping.

2 servings (1¼ cups sauce, with 2 cups vegetables and 4 skewers beef).

Preparation time: 40 minutes.
Ready to serve: 40 minutes.

WALNUT, SAGE AND ONION BREADSTICK TWISTS

Use refrigerated breadsticks as the base for these tasty twists. There's even a bonus serving to eat for lunch the next day.

1 tablespoon butter
¼ cup chopped onion
¼ cup chopped walnuts
1½ teaspoons chopped fresh sage
1 (7-oz.) can refrigerated breadsticks

● Heat oven to 375°F. In medium skillet, melt butter over medium heat. Add onion; sauté 3 to 4 minutes or until tender. Add walnuts and sage; sauté 2 minutes more.

● Unroll breadsticks; press sautéed mixture into dough. Cut along score lines; twist dough. Place on ungreased baking sheet; bake 13 to 15 minutes or until browned.

6 breadsticks.

Preparation time: 15 minutes.
Ready to serve: 30 minutes.

INDIVIDUAL HEART-SHAPED PEAR TARTS WITH CARAMEL SAUCE

Homemade caramel sauce adorns these puff pastry-based tarts. If you're in a real hurry, use store-bought sauce instead.

TART
- **2 frozen puff pastry shells, thawed from (10-oz.) pkg.**
- **1 ripe Bartlett pear**
- **1 tablespoon sugar**
- **⅛ teaspoon ground cinnamon**

CARAMEL SAUCE
- **⅓ cup sugar**
- **2 tablespoons water**
- **⅓ cup hot whipping cream**

● Heat oven to 425°F. Roll puff pastry shells on lightly floured counter to flatten slightly. Fold each circle in half; cut around edges to form half-heart. Unfold; place on parchment-lined baking sheet. Cut pear in half; core and cut in quarters. Cut each quarter into ¼-inch-thick slices; arrange one quarter in fan shape on 1 side of heart. Arrange second quarter on other side; repeat with remaining heart. In small bowl, mix 1 tablespoon sugar and cinnamon; sprinkle over hearts. Bake 20 to 25 minutes or until well browned.

● Meanwhile, in small saucepan, heat ⅓ cup sugar and water over medium heat, stirring constantly. Stop stirring when sugar is dissolved and mixture comes to a boil. Dip pastry brush in dish of cold water; brush sides of pan to wash down any sugar crystals. Continue boiling without stirring until mixture begins to brown. Swirl pan gently to even caramelization. When mixture is rich brown, remove from heat. Immediately add hot cream. (Mixture will bubble up.) Return to low heat; stir to dissolve all caramelized sugar. Serve warm over tarts. (May be made ahead of time. Store covered in refrigerator; reheat before serving.)

2 servings.

Preparation time: 45 minutes.
Ready to serve: 45 minutes.

Valentine Champagne Bucket

Few things say "Valentine's Day" more than pink Champagne, and here's just the container to put it (or the wine for your meal) in. A simple heart-shaped stencil and spray paint transforms a galvanized bucket into Cupid's own wine cooler. If you're in the mood, you can even add a couple of drops of red food coloring to your ice cube tray for pink ice cubes! Add a pink or red napkin as a wrap for the bottle and you've got the perfect gift to carry to your Valentine's Day celebration.

MATERIALS

- **Galvanized bucket**
- **Small cans spray paint, in several shades of red and pink**
- **Heavyweight construction paper**
- **X-acto knife**
- **Medium-point black marking pen**
- **Red napkin**

INSTRUCTIONS

1. Using the X-acto knife, cut heart-shaped stencils in the construction paper. Cut three different-sized stencils.

2. Place the stencil firmly against the bucket to prevent paint from spraying under the stencil. Spray different colors for different-sized heart shapes, overlapping them, if desired.

3. Once dry, outline the hearts, using the black marking pen.

No-Fuss Passover Seder

by Bruce Weinstein

Preparing a kosher house for Passover takes days: changing out dishes; swapping flatware; cleaning the refrigerator, freezer and cupboards. Preparing a Passover Seder can take just as long if you do it from scratch. But there's no need to grind your own white fish to make delectable gefilte fish, boil chicken's feet for a satisfying soup, or stand all day over a simmering brisket. With these recipes, everything can be made ahead, and nothing needs constant attention. Thus you can spend more holiday time with your family. All it takes is a few simple tricks for light-as-air matzo balls, fork-tender brisket and to-die-for macaroons. Think of this menu as a roadmap of shortcuts to an authentic Passover Seder that will have everyone thinking you slaved all day over a hot stove. Your mother-in-law will never know and you'll have plenty of time to enjoy the meal—and each other.

MENU

Trushee (Sephardic Pickled Vegetables)

Doctored Gefilte Fish

Matzo Ball Soup

Slow-Cooker Brisket

Tropical Macaroons

CRAFT

Afikomen Bags

TRUSHEE (SEPHARDIC PICKLED VEGETABLES)

These easy-to-make pickles will last for weeks; even after Passover is finished, you can enjoy them with sandwiches. Serve them as a salad to start a Seder dinner, or alongside the gefilte fish instead of the traditional horseradish.

  1 **lb. green beans, trimmed**
  3 **cups cauliflower florets (about 1 small head)**
  1 **lb. baby carrots, peeled**
12 **fresh sage leaves**
  6 **garlic cloves, quartered**
  3 **cups white vinegar**
  3 **cups water**
  ¼ **cup plus 2 tablespoons sugar**
  2 **tablespoons salt**

● In large pot, bring 4 quarts salted water to a boil over high heat. Add beans; cook 2 minutes. Remove with slotted spoon. Rinse under cold water; drain. Transfer to large bowl.

● Return water to a boil. Add cauliflower; cook 3 minutes. Remove with slotted spoon. Rinse under cold water; drain. Transfer to bowl with beans.

● Return water to a boil. Add carrots; cook 4 minutes. Remove with slotted spoon. Rinse under cold water; drain. Transfer to bowl with beans and cauliflower. Tuck sage and garlic into cool vegetables.

● In large pot, bring vinegar, water, sugar and salt to a boil over high heat. Pour over vegetables; cool to room temperature. Cover; refrigerate 6 hours or up to 3 weeks.

6 servings.

Preparation time: 25 minutes.
Ready to serve: 7 hours, 30 minutes.

Doctored Gefilte Fish

Jarred gefilte fish never tasted as good as your grandmother's made-from-scratch ... until now. By simmering prepared fish quenelles with aromatic herbs and vegetables, gefilte fish takes on a homemade flavor without the bother of grinding your own fish.

1 **medium onion, thinly sliced**
2 **carrots, cut into ¼-inch rounds**
2 **ribs celery, cut into ½-inch pieces**
6 **pieces jarred gefilte fish***
8 **sprigs fresh parsley**
4 **sprigs fresh dill**
4 **cups vegetable broth**
   Lettuce leaves
   Horseradish

● In medium pot, layer onion, carrots, celery, gefilte fish, parsley and dill; cover with broth. Simmer 2 hours over medium-low heat, partially covered.

● Cool to room temperature. Remove fish with slotted spoon; discard vegetables and broth. Cover; refrigerate 3 hours or up to 1 day. Serve on lettuce leaves with horseradish.

TIP *For the best flavor, look for jarred gefilte fish labeled "all white fish."

6 servings.

Preparation time: 10 minutes.
Ready to serve: 5 hours, 10 minutes.

MATZO BALL SOUP

As long as you make your own matzo balls, there's no need to make this soup from scratch. You can doctor good-quality canned chicken broth with vegetables and bouillon cubes to save hours in the kitchen.

MATZO BALLS
- ½ **cup matzo meal**
- ½ **teaspoon salt**
- ½ **teaspoon onion powder**
- ½ **teaspoon baking soda**
- ½ **teaspoon freshly ground white pepper**
- 2 **eggs, lightly beaten**
- 2 **tablespoons vegetable oil**

SOUP
- 2 **quarts reduced-sodium chicken broth**
- 3 **carrots, thinly sliced**
- 2 **ribs celery, thinly sliced**
- 1 **tablespoon chopped fresh dill**
- 1 **bouillon cube* (optional)**

● In medium bowl, mix matzo meal, salt, onion powder, baking soda and white pepper until well combined. Stir in eggs and oil until completely blended. Refrigerate 15 minutes.

● Boil large pot of water over high heat. With wet fingers, roll scant tablespoon batter into ball; gently drop into pot. Repeat with remaining batter. Reduce heat to low; simmer balls 20 minutes, covered.

● Remove matzo balls with slotted spoon; transfer to lipped plate until soup is ready. May be covered and refrigerated up to 24 hours.

● In large pot, bring broth, carrots, celery, dill and bouillon cube, if used, to a boil over high heat; reduce heat to low. Simmer 25 minutes, partially covered.

● Add *Matzo Balls;* heat 5 minutes over low heat.

TIP *Look for "kosher for Passover" bouillon cubes.

6 servings (about 13 cups).

Preparation time: 25 minutes.
Ready to serve: 1 hour.

SLOW-COOKER BRISKET

This is brisket at its easiest. Within hours, your house will fill with the aroma of a beef stew that is rich with sweet potatoes, prunes and onions. The brisket must be well trimmed, so ask your butcher to remove all exterior fat or do it yourself with a sharp knife.

2	**medium russet potatoes**
2	**medium onions, thinly sliced**
2	**garlic cloves, minced**
2	**bay leaves**
4	**lb. first-cut brisket, trimmed of most visible fat**
2	**teaspoons salt**
2	**teaspoons paprika**
½	**teaspoon freshly ground pepper**
3	**medium sweet potatoes, peeled, quartered**
1	**cup pitted dried plums (prunes)**
3	**tablespoons packed light brown sugar**
2	**cups reduced-sodium beef broth**
¼	**cup red wine vinegar**

● Peel and shred potatoes; place in bottom of 5- to 6-quart crockpot with onions, garlic and bay leaves.

● Rub brisket with salt, paprika and pepper; place in crockpot, cutting to fit as necessary. Top with sweet potatoes and dried plums.

● In medium bowl, dissolve brown sugar in broth and vinegar; add to crockpot. Cook on high 5 hours. With long-handled fork, remove meat. Cut against grain into ½-inch slices; return to crockpot. Gently push meat into sauce; cook on high 1½ hours or until meat is fork-tender.

6 servings.

Preparation time: 30 minutes.
Ready to serve: 7 hours.

TROPICAL MACAROONS

Coconut macaroons are a staple at Passover meals because cakes made with flour are not allowed. Shape each macaroon by hand before baking, or use small (1½-oz.) ice cream scoop instead. Line the baking sheet with parchment to make cleanup a snap.

3	**egg whites, at room temperature**
¼	**teaspoon salt**
¾	**cup powdered sugar, sifted**
3	**cups shredded sweetened coconut**
1	**cup sliced almonds, roughly chopped**
½	**cup dried pineapple, finely chopped**
12	**oz. semisweet chocolate chips (optional)**

● Heat oven to 350°F. Line large baking sheet with parchment paper or spray with nonstick cooking spray.

● In large bowl, beat egg whites and salt with electric mixer at high speed until soft peaks form. Reduce speed to low. Add powdered sugar; beat 3 minutes or until mixture is smooth, thick and holds its shape. Fold in coconut, almonds and pineapple.

● Using your hands or 1½-oz. (about 3 tablespoons) ice cream scoop, create 18 balls; place 1 inch apart on baking sheet. Bake 25 minutes or until macaroons are golden brown; cool completely on baking sheet set on wire rack.

● If using, place chocolate chips in medium bowl set over small pan of simmering water or in top of double boiler. Stir until chips melt halfway; remove bowl from hot water. Continue stirring until chips melt completely.

● Line second baking sheet with waxed paper. Dip cooled macaroons into melted chocolate covering them halfway up sides. Place on waxed paper until chocolate sets.

18 macaroons.

Preparation time: 25 minutes.
Ready to serve: 1 hour, 45 minutes.

fikomen Bags

Finding the hidden bag of matzah (the afikomen) at a Passover Seder is one of the joys children hope for ... and a delight for adults to watch. Traditionally only one bag is hidden, but if desired, you can make one bag for each child, with their name on it—either written with felt-tipped pen or with letters cut out of felt and glued to the bag. Each child has to find his or her own special bag, and everyone goes home happy!

MATERIALS

- **1 piece blue felt, at least 8 by 10 inches**
- **Gold cord, approximately 44 inches long**
- **Tape**
- **X-acto knife**

INSTRUCTIONS

1. Cut felt into an 8- by 10-inch rectangle.

2. Fold the felt in two, leaving about 2 inches extra at top to serve as a flap.

3. Using the X-acto knife, make slits all the way through both layers of felt, at about 1-inch intervals.

4. Tape the ends of the cord so it will not fray, and will be easier to push through the holes. Starting at the top, thread the cord up and down through the holes, until they reach the top hole on the opposite side.

5. Cut a hole in the center bottom of the flap. Pull the cord so that both ends are even. Thread both ends through the hole in the flap and tie into a bow.

Easter Sunrise Breakfast

by Mark Scarbrough

Whether you get up before dawn on Easter Sunday or sleep until just before the 11:00 o'clock service, this breakfast will start your holiday right. The flavors here are the essence of springtime—bright, light and intense. And the menu itself is a mélange of old favorites (some long forgotten) and new twists on classics. The best news of all, however, may be that you needn't spend all morning in the kitchen preparing these quick, easy but very sophisticated dishes. Most of them can be prepared ahead of time. Only Shirred Eggs are last minute, but they're so easy, you can pull them together in a few minutes. And that gives you more time with family and friends. That's what Easter is about, anyway.

MENU

Strawberry Banana Smoothie

Shirred Eggs

Low-Fat Lemon Basil Muffins

Canadian Bacon Hash

Melon Salad with Honey Yogurt Dressing

CRAFT

Easter Terra-Cotta Pots

STRAWBERRY BANANA SMOOTHIE

Nothing gets the day going like a silky, creamy smoothie. The trick is all in the ice: Use cubes about 1 inch square. If yours are larger, place them in a plastic bag and hit them once or twice with a mallet or the bottom of a large stockpot. This recipe makes only two servings, but can be doubled or even tripled, depending on the size of your celebration (and your blender). You can also make these smoothies in batches, so they're ready to serve as each person gets out of bed.

- **1 ripe banana**
- **½ cup lemon yogurt (regular, low-fat or nonfat)**
- **½ cup strawberry sorbet**
- **⅓ cup apple juice or white grape juice**
- **⅓ cup ice cubes**
- **1 teaspoon lemon juice**

● In blender, combine banana, yogurt, sorbet, apple juice, ice cubes and lemon juice. Cover; pulse 3 or 4 times. Continue blending on pre-set "blend" or medium speed until creamy, about 1 minute. Pulse as necessary to break up ice. Serve immediately.

2 cups.

Preparation time: 5 minutes.
Ready to serve: 5 minutes.

SHIRRED EGGS

Long out of vogue, this easy but hearty breakfast deserves a comeback. The baked eggs (pronounced "sherd") are a British reinvention of the French classic, "oeufs sur le plat." Unfortunately, direct heat toughens unstabilized egg whites, so a little cream in the dish helps protect those delicate proteins. Ground white pepper is the best choice for seasoning, since it won't put black dots into the creamy whites—but freshly ground black pepper tastes just as good as white.

2	**tablespoons unsalted butter, for greasing cups or ramekins**
¼	**cup heavy cream**
2	**tablespoons finely minced fresh chives**
2	**tablespoons finely chopped fresh tarragon**
6	**eggs, at room temperature**
	Salt and freshly ground pepper

● Heat oven to 350°F. Butter 6 (¾- or 1-cup) custard cups or heatproof ramekins.

● In small saucepan, gently warm cream over very low heat. Do not boil. Stir in chives and tarragon; set aside to steep 30 minutes or up to 3 hours.

● Place 1 teaspoon cream mixture in each custard cup; break egg in each. Divide remaining cream mixture among cups. Season with salt and pepper.

● Place cups on large baking sheet. Bake 8 to 10 minutes or just until whites begin to set; yolks should be runny. Remove from oven; let stand 2 minutes before serving.

6 servings.

Preparation time: 5 minutes.
Ready to serve: 50 minutes.

Low-Fat Lemon Basil Muffins

These creations may not be fat-free, but they're close enough for Easter morning! What's even better, these lemony muffins are laced with basil, that springtime treat, which adds a spicy touch your guests won't expect. Because of the ricotta, these dense muffins are a little chewy, the perfect foil to Shirred Eggs. These muffins won't brown deeply, but instead remain a creamy, yellowy pleasure—good hot out of the oven or later on at room temperature.

 2 cups all-purpose flour
1½ cups sugar
 2 teaspoons baking powder
 1 teaspoon salt
 ½ teaspoon baking soda
 ½ cup low-fat or nonfat buttermilk
 ½ cup low-fat ricotta cheese
 ¼ cup low-fat (1%) or nonfat milk
 3 tablespoons unsalted butter, softened
 2 eggs, at room temperature
 3 tablespoons lemon juice
 1 tablespoon grated lemon peel
 ⅔ cup tightly packed basil leaves, coarsely chopped

● Heat oven to 375°F. Spray 12 medium muffin cups with nonstick cooking spray.

● In medium bowl, stir flour, sugar, baking powder, salt and baking soda until well combined.

● In large bowl, beat buttermilk, ricotta, milk and butter with wire whisk or electric mixer at medium speed. When smooth, beat in eggs, one at a time. Beat in lemon juice, lemon peel and basil just until combined. Stir in dry ingredients with wooden spoon or rubber spatula only until dough is formed—do not overmix. Spoon evenly into muffin cups; do not press down. Bake about 25 minutes or until muffins are set and edges browned. Cool in pan on wire rack 10 minutes; remove from pan. Serve immediately or store covered at room temperature up to 3 days.

12 muffins.

Preparation time: 30 minutes.
Ready to serve: 1 hour, 5 minutes.

CANADIAN BACON HASH

To make this morning main dish, you'll need to have your butcher slice the Canadian bacon ½ inch thick—far thicker than the packaged variety. If you can't get thick Canadian bacon, use smoked ham instead. And use yams, not yellow sweet potatoes—yams are starchier and won't break down so easily. The trick to a good hash is to stir it just enough to keep it moist, but not so much that the potatoes mash. You can make this hash in advance and keep it covered in the refrigerator; then reheat it, covered, in a 350°F oven for 10 minutes.

2   **large red-skinned potatoes, (about ¾ lb.), cut into 1/2-inch pieces**
1   **medium Red Garnet yam or other yam (about ¾ lb.), peeled, cut into ½-inch pieces**
3   **tablespoons unsalted butter**
1   **large red onion, diced**
1   **red bell pepper, diced**
2   **garlic cloves, minced**
¾   **lb. Canadian bacon or smoked ham, cut into ½-inch cubes**
¼   **cup plus 2 tablespoons reduced-sodium chicken or vegetable broth**
2   **tablespoons vegetable oil**
1   **tablespoon caraway seeds**
1   **cup spinach leaves, coarsely chopped**
2   **teaspoons cider vinegar**
1   **teaspoon freshly ground pepper**
½   **teaspoon salt**

● Bring 2 pots salted water to a boil over high heat. In separate pots, cook potatoes and yam 7 minutes. Drain; set aside.

● In large skillet or 14-inch sauté pan, melt 2 tablespoons of the butter over medium-low heat. Cook onion until soft, about 4 minutes, stirring frequently. Add remaining tablespoon butter, bell pepper and garlic. Cook, stirring occasionally, until fragrant, about 2 minutes.

● Increase heat to medium; add Canadian bacon. Sauté, stirring constantly, 1 minute. Add ¼ cup of the broth, oil, caraway seeds and potatoes; cook, stirring frequently but gently, 9 minutes.

● Stir in remaining 2 tablespoons broth, spinach, vinegar, pepper and salt. Cook 3 minutes or until spinach is wilted. Serve immediately or cool, cover and refrigerate up to 2 days.

6 cups.

Preparation time: 40 minutes.
Ready to serve: 50 minutes.

MELON SALAD WITH HONEY YOGURT DRESSING

This dish is Persian in origin, a classic Middle Eastern combination of mint, cumin and ginger. In fact, the dressing might be best made with Greek yogurt, slightly thicker and "cheesier" than other varieties. Melon flesh can be scooped with a melon baller or tiny ice cream scoop. But be forewarned: The balls will weep once dressed. If you want to prepare the salad in advance, keep fruit separate from dressing, tossing them together at the last minute. In fact, the dressing can be made up to one week in advance—and is best if it sits overnight. Store tightly covered in refrigerator.

1 cup vanilla yogurt (regular, low-fat or nonfat)	● In large bowl, stir yogurt, honey, mint, ginger, cumin, salt and hot pepper sauce until well combined. Cover; refrigerate at least 30 minutes or overnight.
2 tablespoons honey	
2 tablespoons chopped fresh mint	
½ teaspoon ground ginger	
½ teaspoon ground cumin	● In large serving bowl, toss melons and green onions with dressing. Serve immediately.
¼ teaspoon salt	
1 to 4 drops hot pepper sauce	
1 (3- to 4-lb.) honeydew melon, seeded, flesh scooped into 1-inch balls	**2 cups.**
1 (2- to 3-lb.) cantaloupe melon, seeded, flesh scooped into 1-inch balls	Preparation time: 30 minutes. Ready to serve: 1 hour.
2 green onions, green part only, minced	

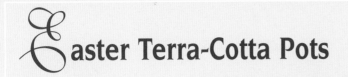aster Terra-Cotta Pots

This project results in a quintessential spring statement: Pastel-colored eggs nestled in a small patch of fresh green growing grass, each in its own small terra-cotta pot. Adding each guest's name on the side of the pot makes the effect even more special, a delightful party favor to take home. Just remember to start this project about ten days before Easter, as the wheat grass will take that long to sprout.

MATERIALS

- 2½-inch terra-cotta pots, one per person
- Correction pen, filled with opaque white ink
- Pencil
- Fine-point black marker
- Potting soil
- Wheat grass seeds (available at nurseries and garden centers)
- Colored Easter eggs

INSTRUCTIONS

1. Using a pencil, write the name of each of your guests onto the rim of a clay pot. Block letters work best.

2. Fill in the outlines of the letters with the white correction pen. Outline with the fine-point black marker.

3. Fill each pot with potting soil to about ½ inch below the rim. Tamp down.

4. Sprinkle wheat grass seeds on top of soil and press down so they are barely covered with soil.

5. Gently sprinkle seeds with water and place on a sunny windowsill. Place an egg on top of soil so grass will grow up around it. Keep soil barely moist. The wheat grass should be about 3 inches tall in 7 to 10 days.

Russian Easter Brunch Celebration

by Colleen Miner

In old Russia, there was no greater celebration than Easter. This menu taps into that wonderful tradition for a contemporary Easter feast of your own. In keeping with today's lifestyle, most of these festive dishes can be prepared ahead, and convenience products make them easy to prepare. But the tastes are authentic, and so wonderful, from the Paskha *(sweet cheese spread)* you'll use on Kulich *(special Easter bread)* … to the fresh salad, delicate blini and wonderful cherry sauce.

MENU

Paskha (Easter Sweet Cheese Spread)

Kulich (Easter Bread)

Chef Salad à la Russe

Blini

Warm Cherry Sauce

CRAFT

Polka-Dot Pillar Candles

PASKHA (EASTER SWEET CHEESE SPREAD)

This deliciously creamy sweetened spread is a traditional Russian Easter favorite. Usually molded into a cone and decorated, paskha tastes just as good served in a pretty bowl. It is the companion to the Easter bread that follows, but will enhance most any breakfast favorite—from toast to bagels to English muffins.

8 oz. cream cheese, at room temperature
¼ cup unsalted butter, at room temperature
⅓ cup sugar
¼ cup cream
½ teaspoon vanilla
¼ cup dried currants
¼ cup chopped toasted almonds
Almonds and raisins, for decorating

● In large bowl, blend cream cheese, butter, sugar, cream and vanilla with electric mixer until smooth. Beat currants and chopped almonds into mixture by hand. Cover; refrigerate until ready to serve.

● To serve the traditional Russian way, wash and dry a new 6-inch medium clay flowerpot (about 2-cup capacity); line with several layers damp cheesecloth, letting about 2 inches hang over rim. Spoon cheese mixture into pot, pressing down to form a solid mass. Fold cheesecloth over top; refrigerate at least 2 hours or overnight. Unmold cheese spread, carefully unwrapping cheesecloth. Decorate with almonds and raisins, traditionally with the letters XB (meaning "Christos Voskress" or "Christ has risen"). Top with a small dove figurine (available at craft stores).

8 servings.

Preparation time: 10 minutes.
Ready to serve: 2 hours, 10 minutes.

KULICH (EASTER BREAD)

The column shape and fancy decoration make this simple fruit-and-nut bread special. It is the perfect accompaniment to the sweet cream cheese Paskha. *Make this bread in a loaf pan and decorate it just like the Russian version.*

1 (1-lb.) loaf frozen bread dough, thawed
½ cup raisins
½ cup slivered almonds, toasted, chopped
1 tablespoon ground cinnamon
2 (28-oz.) tomato cans, labels removed, tomatoes reserved for another use
1 cup powdered sugar
2 tablespoons milk
¼ cup pastel candy sprinkles

● Roll dough out to 12x10-inch rectangle. Sprinkle raisins, almonds and cinnamon evenly over dough. Roll dough up jelly-roll fashion; divide into 2 equal pieces. Knead each section until raisins and almonds are incorporated.

● Place dough into 2 cans that have been cleaned and coated with nonstick cooking spray. Cover; let dough rise in warm place until doubled in volume, about 2 hours.

● Bake on lowest rack of 350°F oven 30 minutes or until internal temperature reaches 200°F. Remove loaves from cans; cool on wire rack.

● Meanwhile, in small bowl, combine powdered sugar and milk to make glaze. When bread is completely cool, pour glaze over domed tops of loaves; sprinkle with candies.

● To serve, cut off dome tops; cut round slices from column. To keep bread fresh, replace dome until ready to serve again.

8 servings.

Preparation time: 15 minutes.
Ready to serve: 2 hours, 45 minutes.

Chef Salad à la Russe

This very traditional American salad takes on a whole new flavor when tossed with traditional Russian ingredients. For those who like to pick and choose their toppings, serve greens in a large bowl surrounded by smaller bowls of toppings.

10 **cups mixed greens**
 4 **hard-cooked eggs, peeled, halved and cut into strips**
 1 **(8.5-oz.) can sliced beets, drained, cut into thin strips**
 4 **oz. sliced ham, cut into thin strips**
 4 **oz. small cooked shrimp**
 4 **oz. blue cheese, crumbled**
 ½ **cup sliced red onion**
 2 **cups plain yogurt or favorite dressing**

● Place greens in large salad bowl; top with eggs, beets, ham, shrimp, blue cheese and red onion. Serve with yogurt.

12 cups.

Preparation time: 20 minutes.
Ready to serve: 20 minutes.

BLINI

These delicate little pancakes are the Russian symbol for the sun—the perfect dish for a sunny Easter brunch. You can make the yeast batter ahead and refrigerate it until it's ready to rise, about one hour before cooking. You can also cook the pancakes ahead and warm them just before serving with Warm Cherry Sauce.

1⅓ **cups all-purpose flour**
 2 **tablespoons sugar**
 2 **teaspoons active dry yeast**
⅛ **teaspoon salt**
1⅓ **cups milk**
¼ **cup butter**
 2 **eggs, beaten**
¼ **cup melted butter, for brushing griddle**

● In large bowl, combine flour, sugar, yeast and salt.

● In glass bowl, heat milk and butter in microwave oven about 45 seconds. Stir until butter is melted. Mixture should be between 105°F and 115°F or warm, but comfortable to the touch. Add milk mixture to dry ingredients; whisk until blended without lumps. Add eggs; continue to blend. Cover bowl; place in warm spot about 45 minutes or until batter doubles.

● Heat large nonstick griddle or frying pan over medium heat; lightly brush with melted butter. Drop batter by heaping tablespoonfuls onto griddle. Cook pancakes about 1 minute or until tops bubble. Turn; cook about 30 seconds or until bottoms are browned. Place pancakes on ovenproof platter; keep warm in 175°F oven until ready to serve.

36 (2-inch) pancakes.

Preparation time: 30 minutes.
Ready to serve: 1 hour, 15 minutes.

WARM CHERRY SAUCE

This sweet, tart sauce tastes like cherry pie without the crust. It is the perfect topping for Blini or your own special pancakes. If you have any of this left over (and that's a big "if"), try drizzling it warm over ice cream.

1 (16-oz.) pkg. frozen cherries, thawed
1 cup sugar
   Grated peel and juice of 1 orange
1 cinnamon stick
2 tablespoons cornstarch
½ cup water

● In medium saucepan, combine cherries, sugar, orange peel, orange juice and cinnamon stick; cook over medium heat until hot, about 3 minutes.

● In small bowl, mix cornstarch and ½ cup water until completely dissolved. Add mixture to hot cherry sauce; continue to heat until sauce thickens, about 1 minute.

3 cups.

Preparation time: 10 minutes.
Ready to serve: 10 minutes.

Polka-Dot Pillar Candles

Polka dots and Easter seem go together like colored eggs and baskets. Ordinary pillar candles can be made extraordinary by simply inserting thumbtacks into their sides. Choose multi-colored thumbtacks or go for a combination of gold and silver. Either way, the sprinkling of round confetti on the table will create a polka dot extravaganza, sure to be remembered, for any Easter celebration.

MATERIALS

- **Pillar candles**
- **Colored thumbtacks**
- **Round confetti**

INSTRUCTIONS

1. Push the thumbtacks into the candles in a pleasing arrangement.

2. Place the candles on the table and toss the confetti around them.

A Patriotic 4th of July

by Michele Anna Jordan

Fourth of July is as good an excuse as any to relax for the day, and share good food with great friends. It is also a wonderful time to celebrate the abundance of America's farms, rivers and seacoasts. To fully enjoy this holiday menu, make the salsa, salad and chutney the day before, prepare the marinade and the melons in the morning, and set out the cheeses just before guests arrive. If you also organize the table in advance, the actual before-dinner work will be minimal. For beverages, offer cold beer and ale, and a chilled dry rosé—a perfect wine in hot weather. This beautiful and taste-filled menu was designed for ten people—a good size for a Fourth of July get-together.

MENU

Firecracker Shrimp

Summer Rice Salad with Heirloom Tomatoes

Grilled Wild Salmon with Corn and Sweet Pepper Salsa

American Artisan Cheeses with Blueberry Chutney and Summer Greens

Tipsy Melons with Mint

CRAFT

Red, White and Blue Luminarias

FIRECRACKER SHRIMP

Serve these fiery shrimp at least an hour before dinner, so your guests can nibble on them leisurely, without having to move on to the next course too quickly.

3 lb. fresh medium shrimp, cleaned but not peeled
1 large garlic bulb, cloves separated, peeled, crushed and minced
½ cup fresh lime juice
2 teaspoons crushed red pepper
¾ teaspoon chipotle powder
2 tablespoons hot pepper sauce of choice
1 teaspoon kosher (coarse) salt, plus more as needed
Freshly ground white pepper
½ cup olive oil
¾ cup butter
Freshly ground pepper

● Put shrimp in large bowl. In small bowl, combine half of the garlic, lime juice, crushed red pepper, chipotle powder, 1 tablespoon of the hot pepper sauce, salt and white pepper. Stir in oil; pour mixture over shrimp, tossing gently but thoroughly. Cover; marinate in refrigerator 2 hours or up to 4 hours, tossing several times.

● To serve, in small saucepan, melt butter. Add remaining garlic and tablespoon hot pepper sauce; season with black pepper. Remove from heat. Pour into warm serving bowl; set in middle of serving platter.

● Drain marinade from shrimp; discard marinade. Heat large nonstick sauté pan over medium-high heat; add handful of shrimp. Cook on 1 side about 90 seconds or until shrimp begin to turn pink. Turn shrimp; cook 1 to 2 minutes more or until just firm and pink throughout. Do not overcook. Season with salt and black pepper; transfer to platter with sauce. Continue until all of the shrimp have been cooked. Serve immediately.

10 servings.

Preparation time: 50 minutes.
Ready to serve: 2 hours, 15 minutes.

SUMMER RICE SALAD WITH HEIRLOOM TOMATOES

Summer farmers' markets offer countless varieties of heirloom tomatoes in a veritable rainbow of colors, from pale yellow and pink to blood red and bright orange. Green grape tomatoes, slightly larger than traditional cherry tomatoes, are sweet and tangy; Sungold cherry tomatoes are nearly as sweet as candy. Choose your favorites to make this salad.

2 cups white rice, such as jasmine or basmati

2 small (5-inch) yellow summer squash, cut into small dice

1 small (5-inch) zucchini, cut into small dice

1 pint small golden cherry tomatoes, cut in half crosswise

1 pint small pear-shaped red cherry tomatoes, cut in half lengthwise

3 tablespoons snipped fresh chives

3 tablespoons minced fresh Italian parsley

3 tablespoons minced fresh basil

1 tablespoon minced fresh oregano
Kosher (coarse) salt to taste, plus 1 teaspoon for dressing
Freshly ground pepper to taste

6 garlic cloves, minced

⅓ cup fresh lemon juice

1 cup extra virgin olive oil

6 large heirloom tomatoes, cut into ¼-inch-thick rounds

6 small heirloom tomatoes, cut into wedges
Sprigs golden and red currant tomatoes

● Cook rice in salted water according to package directions. When cooked, spread over large sheet pan or in large wide bowl to cool.

● When rice has cooled to room temperature, add summer squash, zucchini, cherry tomatoes, chives, parsley, basil and oregano; toss thoroughly. Season with salt and pepper; toss again.

● In small bowl, whisk together garlic, lemon juice and 1 teaspoon salt. Whisk in oil; season generously with pepper. Taste; adjust seasoning and acid balance, adding more lemon juice or oil as needed. Pour dressing over rice salad; toss gently but thoroughly.

● Arrange vegetable mixture on large serving platter; mound rice salad on top. Garnish with heirloom and currant tomatoes. Season with salt and pepper. Salad can rest at room temperature up to 1 hour before serving.

10 servings.

Preparation time: 50 minutes.
Ready to serve: 1 hour, 35 minutes.

VARIATION To make this salad a day ahead, pour just half of the dressing over the salad and toss thoroughly. Cover with plastic wrap; refrigerate until 45 minutes before serving. Cover and refrigerate remaining dressing as well; removing 45 minutes before serving with the salad. Do not cut larger tomatoes until then.

GRILLED WILD SALMON WITH CORN AND SWEET PEPPER SALSA

Farmed salmon is available year-round, but it lacks the rich flavor and firm texture of wild Pacific King salmon, which is generally available May through September. It is worth the effort it takes to find.

1 tablespoon kosher (coarse) salt
1 teaspoon chipotle powder
2 large wild King salmon fillets (about 2½ to 3 lb. each), scaled, cut into 10 equal (by weight) pieces
1 bunch fresh cilantro, trimmed
Freshly ground pepper
Corn and Sweet Pepper Salsa (page 73)
2 limes, cut into wedges

● Prepare charcoal fire in outdoor grill or heat stove-top grill to medium. Combine salt and chipotle powder; rub it over cut surface of fillets. Grill, cut-side down, about 8 minutes, rotating once to mark it. Turn salmon; grill until fish begins to flake, 2 to 3 minutes for 1-inch fillet, longer if fish is thicker.

● Spread cilantro over large serving platter; top with salmon, leaving room in center for bowl of salsa. Grind a little black pepper over salmon. Spoon a little salsa on top of each fillet; place lime wedges between fillets. Put remaining salsa in small serving bowl; set in center of platter.

8 to 10 servings.

Preparation time: 25 minutes.
Ready to serve: 25 minutes.

Corn and Sweet Pepper Salsa

1 large or 2 medium red bell peppers
3 to 4 ears corn, shucked
1 small red onion, minced
2 serranos, minced
¼ teaspoon chipotle powder
   Grated peel of 3 limes
   Kosher (coarse) salt
   Freshly ground pepper
⅓ cup fresh lime juice
½ cup unrefined corn oil or mild olive oil
⅓ cup minced fresh cilantro

● Grill bell peppers: Put them on rack set above hot coals; turn frequently until their skins are evenly blackened. Put peppers in bowl; cover with tea towel. Let cool until they are easy to handle. Use your fingers to remove all of the blackened peel. Cut off stem; remove seed core. Cut peppers in half lengthwise. Remove any large inner ribs; cut peppers into ¼-inch-wide strips. Cut strips crosswise into ¼-inch dice. Put diced peppers in medium mixing bowl.

● Grill corn on edges of charcoal fire, turning frequently, until it barely begins to color, about 3 minutes. Set aside to cool. Using sharp knife, cut corn from cob; put in bowl with peppers. Add onion, serranos, chipotle powder and lime peel; toss gently. Season with salt and pepper. Stir in lime juice, oil and cilantro. Taste; adjust seasoning. Cover; set aside until ready to serve. (Refrigerate if salsa will be held more than 1 hour; remove from refrigerator 30 minutes before serving. Stir salsa; taste. Adjust seasoning if needed immediately before serving.)

About 4 cups.

Preparation time: 1 hour.
Ready to serve: 1 hour.

AMERICAN ARTISAN CHEESES WITH BLUEBERRY CHUTNEY AND SUMMER GREENS

Scores of hand-crafted artisan cheeses are made in America today, some of which are good enough to rival the famous cheeses of Europe. You don't need to serve all the specific cheeses listed here. Rather, talk to the cheesemonger at the best local cheese department, or shop about for what is best at the time.

1½ cups *Blueberry Chutney* (page 75)
  8 oz. Vella Dry Jack cheese
  8 oz. cheddar cheese
  8 oz. teleme or fromage blanc cheese
  6 oz. Pt. Reyes Original blue or Maytag blue cheese
  1 (5-oz.) log fresh soft goat cheese, such as chabis
10 cups fresh young salad greens
    Kosher (coarse) salt
  3 tablespoons extra-virgin olive oil
    Freshly ground pepper

● First, make chutney, preferably at least 1 day before serving.

● Remove all of the cheeses, except fromage blanc, from refrigerator 2 to 3 hours before serving.

● To serve, arrange cheeses on large wooden or marble board. Put chutney in small bowl; set on board. In salad bowl, toss greens with 3 or 4 generous pinches of salt. Add oil; toss again. Add pepper; toss once more. Serve immediately, alongside cheeses.

10 servings.

Preparation time: 10 minutes.
Ready to serve: 10 minutes, plus time to make chutney.

Blueberry Chutney

3 to 4 cups fresh blueberries, rinsed
   2 ripe pears, preferably Comice, peeled, cored and diced
   1 small onion, cut into small dice
   2 jalapeño chiles, stemmed, seeded and minced
     3-inch-piece fresh ginger, peeled, grated
  ¾ cup sugar
   1 teaspoon kosher (coarse) salt
  ½ teaspoon ground cloves
  ⅛ teaspoon ground cardamom
     Dash ground cinnamon
     Dash cayenne pepper
  ¾ cup sherry vinegar or apple cider vinegar

● In heavy medium saucepan, combine blueberries and pears; add onion, jalapeños, ginger, sugar, salt, cloves, cardamom, cinnamon and cayenne. Stir gently. Pour vinegar over mixture; set over medium heat, stirring continuously until liquid boils. Reduce heat to low; simmer until mixture thickens, about 25 minutes. Remove from heat; cool. Transfer to glass jars. Refrigerate up to 2 weeks.

About 4 cups.

Preparation time: 15 minutes.
Ready to serve: 40 minutes.

TIPSY MELONS WITH MINT

The best place to find excellent melons is a local farmers' market. There are so many varieties available. Golden watermelons, which have become increasingly available in the U.S., are almost always sweeter than red; use them if you can find them. Do not use seedless watermelons, as they are grown for their ability to produce few seeds—not for their flavor. If you like, you can cut the watermelon decoratively and use it as a serving bowl for the melon.

2 or 3 **small to medium-size ripe muskmelons (cantaloupe, Charantais, Sharlyn or other variety)**

1 **small to medium-size ripe Crenshaw melon**

1 **small to medium-size ripe Casaba melon**

1 **medium-size ripe watermelon, preferably golden**

1 **cup best-quality tequila**

⅓ **cup simple syrup***

¼ **cup Cointreau (orange liqueur) Juice of 2 limes**

¾ **teaspoon kosher (coarse) salt**

½ **cup fresh mint, cut into very thin crosswise strips**

● Halve muskmelons, Crenshaw and Casaba. Remove and discard seeds; cut each half into 3 or 4 wedges. Peel wedges; cut melon flesh into 1-inch cubes. Put cubes in large serving bowl.

● Cut watermelon in half lengthwise. Make lengthwise cuts, cutting all the way to but not through rind, about 1 inch apart. Repeat, making crosswise cuts. Cut around edge of melon so most of the flesh loosens (cut out the part that doesn't). Transfer watermelon to wide bowl. Cut watermelon strips into 1-inch cubes, removing seeds; add to bowl with other melons.

● Strain watermelon juice that remains in wide bowl; discard seeds. Stir tequila, simple syrup, Cointreau, lime juice and salt into juice; pour over melons, tossing gently. Cover; refrigerate until chilled.

● Just before serving, toss mint with melon. Transfer melon and all of its juices to large serving bowl; serve immediately.

TIP *To make simple syrup: In saucepan bring 2 parts sugar and 1 part water to a boil; reduce heat. Simmer 3 minutes; cool.

8 to 10 servings.

Preparation time: 35 minutes.
Ready to serve: 2 hours, 35 minutes.

$\mathcal{R}$ed, White and Blue Luminarias

These luminarias, made from white lunch bags decorated with red and blue tissue paper, are just the thing to line the path leading to your Fourth of July party. Alternatively, use these light-filled creations as tabletop decorations to put everyone in a festive mood. Even though the bottoms of the sacks are filled with sand, for safety's sake it's best to contain the votive candles in individual glass holders.

MATERIALS

- **White lunch sacks**
- **Red and blue tissue paper**
- **X-acto knife**
- **Spray adhesive or craft glue**
- **Sand**
- **Votive candles and holders**

INSTRUCTIONS

1. Using the X-acto knife, cut sections of the blue and red tissue paper into star and stripe shapes.

2. Lay the cutouts flat on several sections of newspaper and mist lightly with spray adhesive.

3. Position the tissue paper cutout on the paper bags and press firmly into position.

4. Fill the bottoms of the bags with approximately 1½ inches of sand. Place the votive candles into their glass holders and place one in the middle of each bag, pressing them slightly into the sand.

A Family Halloween Gathering

by Cort Sinnes

This menu was developed over time as a means of trying to keep everyone—from young goblins to old witches and ogres—happy on a fun, action-packed holiday. Traditionally, we start the evening with a kids-only Halloween party (complete with a very simple kids' menu—usually home-delivered cheese pizza and apple cider), take the little pranksters trick-or-treating and then serve chili and fixings to the parents when they come to pick up their kids. A decidedly casual affair, we usually serve the chili in mugs, standing in the kitchen, while the young ones run off the effect of too much candy and almost enough fun.

MENU

Classic Chili

Steamed Rice with Chopped Peanuts and Cilantro

Cheesy-Jalapeño Corn Breads

Orange and Red Onion Salad

Pumpkin-Gingerbread with Whipped Cream and Crystallized Ginger

CRAFT

Flying Halloween Bats

CLASSIC CHILI

This is an excellent recipe for chili, one that young and old seem to enjoy. Although it's perfectly acceptable to use ground beef, I much prefer beef stew meat, cut into bite-size pieces. This is one of those dishes that gets better over time, so it can be made a day or two ahead and refrigerated until ready to serve. It also freezes very well.

1½	lb. stew meat (cut into ¾-inch pieces) or ground beef
2	medium onions, finely chopped
2	tablespoons diced green bell pepper
2	garlic cloves, pressed
1	(28-oz.) can diced tomatoes
1	(6-oz.) can tomato paste
1	cup water
1	beef bouillon cube
1	(15- to 16-oz.) can kidney beans, undrained
2 to 3	teaspoons chili powder (hot or mild)
2	teaspoons salt
1 to 2	teaspoons dried oregano
1	teaspoon ground cumin
½	teaspoon crushed red pepper
1	bay leaf
1	cup beer

TOPPINGS

Chopped fresh cilantro
Grated cheddar cheese
Sour cream
Bottled hot pepper sauces

In nonstick Dutch oven or large saucepan, brown meat, onions, bell pepper and garlic over medium-high heat; drain fat. Add tomatoes, tomato paste, water, bouillon, beans, chili powder, salt, oregano, cumin, crushed red pepper, bay leaf and beer; stir to blend. Cover; bring to a simmer. Cook 1½ hours, stirring occasionally. Remove bay leaf. Serve with favorite toppings.

10 cups.

Preparation time: 30 minutes.
Ready to serve: 2 hours.

STEAMED RICE WITH CHOPPED PEANUTS AND CILANTRO

I, for one, love the combination of chili and steamed rice, served in the same bowl or mug or on the side. Chopped peanuts and cilantro add a little salt and spice to the bland rice, perfect for pairing with the complex flavors of the chili.eat for lunch the next day.

3	**cups water**
1	**teaspoon salt**
1½	**cups long-grain white rice**
¼	**cup fresh cilantro, finely chopped**
2 to 3	**tablespoons salted peanuts, chopped**

● In heavy-bottomed saucepan with snug-fitting lid, bring water and salt to a boil. Add rice; stir. Return to a boil. Immediately reduce heat to simmer; cover. Simmer 15 minutes. Remove from heat; allow rice to continue steaming 5 to 10 minutes without removing lid.

● Add cilantro and peanuts; gently fluff rice with fork.

5 cups.

Preparation time: 10 minutes.
Ready to serve: 35 minutes.

CHEESY-JALAPEÑO CORN BREADS

Corn bread and chili go together like the proverbial horse-and-carriage. If time is running short, you can substitute boxed corn bread mix; simply add diced jalapeño chiles and grated cheese to the mix and bake as directed, adding a few minutes to baking time.

1 tablespoon shortening
1¼ cups stone-ground cornmeal
¾ cup all-purpose flour
1 tablespoon sugar
2 teaspoons baking powder
½ teaspoon baking soda
½ teaspoon salt
2 eggs
⅔ cup milk
⅔ cup buttermilk
2 tablespoons butter, melted
1 (4-oz.) can diced jalapeño chiles, drained
1 cup (4 oz.) medium-sharp cheddar cheese, grated

● Heat oven to 425°F. Grease 9x9-inch pan (or 9-inch round cast-iron skillet) with shortening; allow to heat in oven while mixing batter.

● In large bowl, mix together cornmeal, flour, sugar, baking powder, baking soda and salt. In separate bowl, whisk together eggs, milk and buttermilk. Add wet ingredients to dry; stir lightly, folding in butter, jalapeños and cheese once batter is moist. Pour batter into hot pan (batter will be thin.) Bake until toothpick inserted in center comes out clean, 20 to 25 minutes. Serve warm.

9 servings.

Preparation time: 15 minutes.
Ready to serve: 40 minutes.

ORANGE AND RED ONION SALAD

Never had an orange and red onion salad? Give it a try! It's a delightful combination of flavors, perfect for this menu and beautiful to boot.

DRESSING
  1 cup mild vegetable oil, such as canola
  ¼ cup rice wine vinegar
  ¼ cup fresh lemon juice
  ¼ cup finely chopped fresh cilantro
  ½ teaspoon sugar
  Dash salt

SALAD
  6 oranges
  1 medium red onion

● In jar with tight-fitting lid, combine oil, vinegar, lemon juice, cilantro, sugar and salt; shake well. Taste; adjust seasonings. Use at once or cover and refrigerate.

● To assemble salad: Peel oranges; slice into ¼-inch rounds. Cut onion into ⅛-inch slices; separate into rings. On large platter, arrange orange and onion slices in an alternating pattern. Drizzle with dressing; serve at once.

6½ cups.

Preparation time: 30 minutes.
Ready to serve: 30 minutes.

PUMPKIN-GINGERBREAD WITH WHIPPED CREAM AND CRYSTALLIZED GINGER

Gingerbread is another one of those old-fashioned treats perfect for the first chilly nights of autumn. Adding pumpkin lends complementary flavor that is particularly appropriate for a Halloween celebration.

2½ cups unbleached all-purpose flour
 ½ cup whole wheat flour
 1 cup sugar
1½ teaspoons ground ginger
 1 teaspoon ground cinnamon
 1 teaspoon ground nutmeg
 ½ teaspoon ground cloves
 ¼ teaspoon freshly ground pepper
 ¾ cup unsalted butter, cut into 12 pieces
 1 (16-oz.) can pumpkin
 ½ cup light molasses
 ⅓ cup buttermilk
 2 eggs, lightly beaten
    Grated peel of 1 lemon
1½ teaspoons baking soda
    Whipped cream
    Crystallized ginger, coarsely chopped

● Heat oven to 350°F. Grease Bundt pan. In large mixing bowl, combine all-purpose and whole wheat flours, sugar, ground ginger, cinnamon, nutmeg, cloves and pepper. Using food processor or electric mixer, cut in butter until mixture resembles coarse crumbs.

● In separate bowl, whisk together pumpkin, molasses, buttermilk, eggs, lemon peel and baking soda. Stir pumpkin mixture into dry ingredients until just moistened, taking care not to overmix.

● Pour batter into pan. Bake until top is firm to the touch and cake tester inserted into center comes out clean, about 1 hour 20 minutes. Cool on wire rack.

● Top slices of warm gingerbread with whipped cream; sprinkle with crystallized ginger.

8 to 10 servings.

Preparation time: 20 minutes.
Ready to serve: 1 hour, 40 minutes.

Flying Halloween Bats

These black bats, with their bamboo skewer "fangs," are just the thing to twirl above a Halloween buffet table. Candles, set a safe distance directly below them, will ensure they dance through the air all night long.

MATERIALS
- Small and large egg-shaped Styrofoam forms
- Black acrylic paint
- Small paintbrush
- Small plastic "wiggle" eyes
- Black construction paper
- Pencil
- X-acto knife
- Bamboo skewers
- Fine wire
- Black thread
- Thumbtacks

INSTRUCTIONS

1. Paint both the large and small Styrofoam eggs with black acrylic paint. Allow to dry.

2. To make the fangs, cut the sharp tips (approximately ¾ inch long) off of two bamboo skewers. Push into place, side by side, on the small egg shape.

3. Glue the eyes above the fangs.

4. Attach the small egg shape to the large egg shape, using a 1¼-inch-long section of bamboo skewer.

5. Using the pencil, draw the bat wing shape in the middle of one piece of black construction paper. Cut out using the X-acto knife. The wings should be approximately 7 inches long by 2½ inches wide. Use the original bat shape as a pattern for the other wings.

6. Glue a bamboo skewer to the top edge of each wing, leaving approximately 1 inch of the skewer past the end of the wing to attach (to the body of the bat).

7. Cut fine wire (or a paper clip, if need be) into ¾-inch lengths. Bend in half to form a U-shape. Press one into the top of the bat's head and one into the top of his body, leaving enough of the wire "U" to easily pass thread through.

8. Tie black thread to the "U's" as shown in the photo. Cut thread slightly longer than the length you need to hang properly from the ceiling. Tie the loose end of the thread to a thumbtack. Push the thumbtack into the ceiling and adjust to the proper height.

The Colors of Halloween

by Michele Anna Jordan

S o many adults name Halloween as their favorite holiday—you'd think there would be more emphasis on the meal rather than just the trick-or-treating that children so enjoy. This menu celebrates the ancient holiday with spicy fare inspired by Mexico, where Días de los Muertos, or Days of the Dead, is celebrated November 1 and 2, a festival in which people of all ages participate. Elaborate altars honor departed loved ones, and are often filled with their favorite foods, along with candy skulls and cookies shaped like bones. It is a colorful and exuberant celebration. Take time to decorate your table similarly, with orange-red marigolds—the traditional flower of the holiday—candles, a tablecloth made of Mexican oilcloth, and the Halloween hurricane lamp described at the end of the menu. Virgin's Tears, a beverage made of red beets, is traditional in Mexico; you can easily duplicate its rich scarlet color with hibiscus flower tea. Cold beer or a lighter red wine, such as a California pinot noir or Italian dolcetto, is also a good choice.

MENU

Individual Queso Fundido with Black Chanterelles

Butternut Squash Soup with Black Beans and Chipotles

Slow-Roasted Pork with Braised Garlic and Fennel

Full Moon Polenta with Shaved Black Truffles

Langues des Chats with Black Licorice Ice Cream and Blood Sauce

CRAFT

Halloween Hurricane Lamp

INDIVIDUAL QUESO FUNDIDO WITH BLACK CHANTERELLES

Black chanterelles are also known as trompets des morts, *or trumpets of death, making them an ideal starter for a Halloween meal. They are among the most delicate and delicious of all wild mushrooms.*

4	**oz. dried black chanterelle or porcini mushrooms**
3	**tablespoons mild olive oil**
8	**green onions, trimmed, cut into very thin rounds**
6	**garlic cloves, minced**
	Kosher (coarse) salt
	Freshly ground pepper
10	**oz. Monterey Jack cheese, grated**
6	**oz. cheddar cheese, grated**
4	**oz. queso cotija or feta cheese, crumbled**
⅛ to ¼	**teaspoon chipotle powder**
	Blue corn chips (readily available in most markets)

● Put mushrooms in medium bowl; add just enough hot water to cover. Set aside 30 minutes or until mushrooms are fully rehydrated and soft. Strain liquid, reserving it to use in soup or sauce.

● In small sauté pan, heat oil over medium heat. Add half of the green onions; sauté until they just begin to soften, about 3 minutes. Add one-third of the garlic; sauté 30 seconds. Season with salt and pepper; add mushrooms. Sauté 7 minutes or until mushrooms are very limp and flavorful. Remove from heat.

● Heat oven to 375°F.

● In large bowl, toss together cheeses, remaining green onions, remaining garlic and chipotle powder. Divide mixture among individual 4-inch ramekins; set filled ramekins on sheet pan. Bake until cheese is completely melted and bubbly, 10 to 12 minutes. Spoon mushroom mixture over cheese; bake 5 minutes more.

● Set each ramekin on small plate; surround with corn chips. Serve immediately with extra corn chips.

4 servings.

Preparation time: 45 minutes.
Ready to serve: 1 hour.

BUTTERNUT SQUASH SOUP WITH BLACK BEANS AND CHIPOTLES

The colors of Halloween make this soup as hauntingly beautiful as it is flavorful. If you have black soup plates, all the better. You can easily make this soup the day before; just store the black beans separately and heat them thoroughly before adding to reheated soup.

¾ **cup dried black beans, soaked in water overnight, drained**
3 **garlic cloves, unpeeled**
1 **small celery rib**
½ **bay leaf**
½ **onion**
1 **dried whole chipotle chile**
1 **teaspoon kosher (coarse) salt, plus more as needed**
 Freshly ground pepper
3 **tablespoons olive oil**
½ **onion, diced**
1 **jalapeño chile, peeled, seeded and minced**
2 **garlic cloves, minced**
1 **teaspoon ground cumin**
½ **teaspoon chipotle powder**
2 **lb. peeled, cubed butternut squash or other winter squash such as kabocha, delicata, skuri or acorn**
2 **cups reduced-sodium chicken broth**
2½ **cups water, plus more as needed**
½ **cup crème fraîche**

● Put drained beans in medium soup pot; add water to come 1 inch above beans. Add garlic cloves, celery, bay leaf, half onion, whole chipotle, 1 teaspoon salt and pepper; bring to a boil. Reduce heat; simmer uncovered, stirring occasionally, until beans are tender, about 40 minutes. Add water as needed. When beans are tender, remove and discard garlic, celery, bay leaf, onion and chipotle. Set aside.

● In soup pot, heat oil over medium-low heat. Sauté diced onion and jalapeño until limp, 8 to 10 minutes. Add minced garlic, cumin and chipotle powder; sauté 2 minutes. Season with salt and pepper; add squash, broth and 2½ cups water. Bring to a boil. Reduce heat; simmer covered until squash is tender, 30 to 35 minutes. Puree squash in blender.

● Pour soup through strainer into clean saucepan, pressing through as much pulp as possible. Drain beans, reserving cooking liquid. Stir beans into soup; if soup is thick, add reserved cooking liquid and water. Ladle into shallow soup plates. In small bowl, stir crème fraîche several times to loosen; season with salt and pepper. Swirl a spoonful into each soup plate.

9 cups.

Preparation time: 30 minutes.
Ready to serve: 1 hour.

SLOW-ROASTED PORK WITH BRAISED GARLIC AND FENNEL

When an appropriately fatty cut of pork is cooked slowly, it becomes meltingly rich and flavorful, and much of the fat renders out to be poured off before it is served. Do not substitute pork loin, as it will be much too dry. Hawaiian alaea salt is a pale orange salt that is both beautiful and flavorful.

3 tablespoons kosher (coarse) salt
4- to 5-lb. boneless pork shoulder or butt
6 garlic bulbs, outer skins removed
6 medium fennel bulbs, trimmed
Freshly ground pepper
Hawaiian alaea salt, lightly crushed
Lemon wedges

● If you have a clay roaster, soak it according to manufacturer's directions.

● Rub all of the kosher salt into pork. Place pork in clay roaster or roasting pan; add 1 cup water. Put in cold oven. Set heat to 300°F; bake covered 2 hours. Remove pan from oven; add garlic and fennel. Return pan to oven; bake covered 1½ hours or until garlic and fennel are completely tender and pork falls apart when pressed.

● Drain fat that has collected in pan. Cover pork and vegetables. Let rest 10 minutes. Use 2 forks to pull pork into big chunks. Set on platter; surround with garlic and fennel. Season with pepper and alaea salt; garnish with lemon wedges.

6 servings.

Preparation time: 15 minutes.
Ready to serve: 4 hours.

FULL MOON POLENTA WITH SHAVED BLACK TRUFFLES

This dish evokes images of the full moon, emerging from the fog and partially obscured by bats in flight. Here, the bats are represented by thin shavings of black truffles.

8 cups water, plus more as needed
1¼ cups coarse-ground polenta
2 teaspoons kosher (coarse) salt, plus more as needed
2 tablespoons butter, cut into small pieces
6 oz. Parmigiano-Reggiano, Dry Jack or aged Asiago cheese, grated
Freshly ground pepper
¼ cup black truffle oil
1 small fresh black truffle, very thinly shaved*

● In large heavy pot, bring 4 cups of the water to a rolling boil. In smaller pot, bring remaining 4 cups water to a rolling bowl; reduce heat so water just simmers.

● Using whisk, stir water in larger pot in circular direction to create a vortex; slowly pour polenta and 2 teaspoons salt in thin, steady stream into vortex, stirring constantly. Reduce heat; simmer, stirring until all of the polenta has been added and it begins to thicken, 10 to 15 minutes. Replace whisk with wooden spoon; stir in 2 cups of the simmering water. If any lumps have formed, use back of spoon to press them against side of pot.

● Continue to stir polenta, reaching down into bottom of pot, until it is thick, creamy and pulls away from side of pot. Add more water as needed to maintain medium-thick consistency. After 20 minutes, carefully taste polenta; it is done when individual grains are fully tender. Polenta cooks in 20 to 60 minutes, depending on age and size of grains.

● When polenta is almost completely tender, stir in butter and cheese; cook 10 minutes more, stirring constantly. Taste; adjust seasoning. Pour polenta into wide (2-quart)

serving dish, preferably dark blue or black. Drizzle truffle oil over polenta; scatter shaved truffle on top. Cover with tea towel or cloth napkin. Let rest 10 minutes in center of dining table. After guests are seated, remove towel; rising steam will resemble fog clearing from a full moon.

TIP *Although the more flavorful white truffle is in season late October, this recipe calls for black for obvious reasons.

5 (1-cup) servings.

Preparation time: 30 minutes.
Ready to serve: 1 hour, 20 minutes.

LANGUES DES CHATS WITH BLACK LICORICE ICE CREAM AND BLOOD SAUCE

It is easiest to buy ready-made licorice ice cream at your local ice cream parlor.

BLACK LICORICE ICE CREAM AND BLOOD SAUCE
- **1 pint black licorice ice cream**
- **1 cup fresh red raspberries**
- **2 teaspoons superfine sugar**
- **2 teaspoons fresh lemon juice**
- **1 pkg. black licorice shoestring whips**

LANGUES DES CHATS (COOKIES)
- **½ cup unsalted butter, plus more for baking sheet, at room temperature**
- **1 cup sifted powdered sugar**
- **2 eggs, plus 1 egg white**
- **1 teaspoon vanilla**
- **¾ teaspoon finely ground white pepper**
- **½ teaspoon kosher (coarse) salt**
- **⅛ teaspoon cayenne pepper**
- **1 cup all-purpose flour, plus more for baking sheet**

● For ice cream: Set out 6 glass dessert glasses; divide ice cream among glasses. Set glasses in freezer until frosty.

● Put berries in blender or food processor; add sugar and lemon juice. Pulse until smooth. Strain berries; discard seeds. Chill.

● Set glasses on small plates; wrap 2 or 3 licorice whips around each stem. Drizzle each scoop ice cream with raspberry puree. Arrange several cookies on each plate.

● For cookies: Heat oven to 400°F. If using nonstick baking sheet, do not butter or flour the sheet. Otherwise, rub baking sheet with butter and dust with flour.

● In medium glass or stainless steel bowl, beat ½ cup butter with wooden spoon until smooth, creamy and very pale. Beat in powdered sugar. Add eggs, one at a time, followed by egg white, beating after each addition until mixture is smooth. Add vanilla, white pepper, salt and cayenne; beat thoroughly. Beat in 1 cup flour until mixture is very smooth.

● Fit large pastry bag with 5/16-inch round pastry tip; fill bag with batter. Pipe batter onto baking sheet, making strips 2½-inches long and about ⅜-inch wide in center, a bit wider at top and bottom to resemble small bones or dumbbells. Cookies should be 1½ to 2 inches apart.

● Bake 6 to 8 minutes or until edges of cookies begin to turn golden but centers are still pale. Carefully transfer cookies to wire rack to cool completely.

About ⅓ cup sauce, 6 dozen cookies.

Preparation time: 30 minutes.
Ready to serve: 50 minutes.

Halloween Hurricane Lamp

Once you light the candles, these open-ended glass cylinders, covered with autumn leaves, look almost like natural stained-glass windows. If fall foliage is in short supply in your neighborhood, artificial leaves are a good alternative. Attach the leaves using either craft glue or candle adhesive (a special sticky wax that does not harden, made especially for holding candles in holders, available at most variety and craft stores); the benefit of using the candle adhesive is that the leaves can be removed after the holiday and the glass cylinders re-used for other purposes. Choose orange or black candles to create the best Halloween effect.

MATERIALS

- **Glass cylinders, open at both ends**
- **Fresh or artificial autumn leaves**
- **Craft glue or candle adhesive**
- **Pillar candles, preferably orange or black**

INSTRUCTIONS

1. Add several dots of glue to the back side of leaves and press firmly against the glass cylinder. If using candle adhesive, roll wax into pea-sized balls and place several on the back sides of the leaves, then press the leaves into place. For best effect, overlap the leaves.

2. Once the glass cylinders have been completely encircled with leaves, place on table, insert the pillar candles, and light.

Thanksgiving Day Breakfast

by Melanie Barnard

It's the eternal Thanksgiving Dinner dilemma. Will we go to his family or hers? Do we rush from the bird at one table to the pie at another? Or, worst-case scenario, do we have to do the whole thing twice? Here's the answer: Invite some family or friends for a festive Thanksgiving breakfast, and go to their house for dinner. We've included all the traditional flavors in this hearty, yet easy-to-prepare, breakfast. It will sustain you until the big meal, but is light enough to enjoy earlier that same day.

Wake guests up with Cranberry Shrub, then entice them to the table with the aroma of Spiced Warm Apple Compote. Hold their attention with Pumpkin Muffins with Maple Pecan Butter. The creamy eggs and sausage "scrapple" will have them seated, napkins-on-lap, in no time. Best of all, the muffins, flavored butter and compote can all be made a day ahead, giving you precious extra time if you are also charged with stuffing the bird for later in the day.

And note that this special breakfast is a lovely way to turn any late autumn morning (not just Thanksgiving) into a family celebration.

MENU

Cranberry Shrub

Cream Cheese and Chive Scrambled Eggs

Turkey Sausage "Scrapple"

Pumpkin Muffins with Maple Pecan Butter

Spiced Warm Apple Compote

CRAFT

Decorated Note Cards

CRANBERRY SHRUB

Whether using wine or not, this is a refreshing starter for breakfast. This beverage can also serve as a wonderful, seasonal cocktail preceding the big dinner.

1 **(12-oz.) can frozen cranberry juice concentrate, thawed**
2 **cups Riesling or other white wine or ginger ale, chilled**
3 **cups seltzer or club soda, chilled**
   Ice cubes
4 **small scoops lemon or orange sorbet**

● In pitcher, stir together juice concentrate and wine; gently stir in seltzer. Fill 4 tall glasses with ice cubes; pour in cranberry mixture. Add small scoop sorbet to each. Serve with long spoons and straws, if desired.

4 servings.

Preparation time: 5 minutes.
Ready to serve: 5 minutes.

CREAM CHEESE AND CHIVE SCRAMBLED EGGS

Cream cheese is the secret ingredient to ultra-moist scrambled eggs that stay fluffy and tender if serving buffet-style—up to 30 minutes in a covered chafing dish. If you can't find chives at this time of year, use finely chopped green onions.

8 **large eggs**
3 **tablespoons milk**
½ **teaspoon salt**
¼ to ½ **teaspoon freshly ground pepper**
2 **tablespoons butter**
2 **tablespoons (1 oz.) regular or reduced-fat cream cheese, cut into small pieces**
2 **tablespoons snipped fresh chives**

● In mixing bowl, use fork or whisk to combine eggs, milk, salt and pepper until well blended, but not foamy.

● In large skillet, heat butter over medium heat until it begins to sizzle. Reduce heat to medium-low; pour in eggs. Cook, stirring slowly and constantly with wooden spoon or spatula, until soft curds begin to form, 1 to 2 minutes. Add cream cheese; continue cooking and stirring until soft fluffy curds form, 3 to 6 minutes more. Stir in chives.

4 servings.

Preparation time: 15 minutes.
Ready to serve: 15 minutes.

TURKEY SAUSAGE "SCRAPPLE"

Scrapple is a traditional breakfast meat popular in Philadelphia and nearby Pennsylvania Dutch communities. It got its name because it was usually made with scraps of meat and lots of pepper, then held together with cornmeal or other "mush." Fried in butter, scrapple becomes a sort of sausage patty. Here, we start with good turkey or pork breakfast sausage, season generously, dredge in cornmeal and pan-fry. This is modern scrapple—but definitely not made with scraps!

12 oz. turkey or pork breakfast sausage, bulk or links
1½ tablespoons finely chopped fresh sage
¾ teaspoon poultry seasoning
2 tablespoons yellow cornmeal
1 teaspoon freshly ground pepper
1 tablespoon butter, if using turkey sausage

● If using sausage links, squeeze meat from casings. In mixing bowl, use your hands to mix sausage, sage and poultry seasoning. On small plate, combine cornmeal and pepper. Divide sausage mixture into 8 pieces; form each into small patty about ½ inch thick. Dredge patties in cornmeal, turning to coat both sides. (Recipe can be prepared to this point up to 2 hours ahead; refrigerate sausages in single layer.)

● If using turkey sausage, heat butter in large skillet until sizzling. (If using pork sausage, just heat skillet.) Cook sausage patties over medium heat, turning once, until golden brown and cooked through, 5 to 8 minutes. Serve hot.

4 servings.

Preparation time: 10 minutes.
Ready to serve: 20 minutes.

PUMPKIN MUFFINS WITH MAPLE PECAN BUTTER

Extra muffins freeze well, but they are also excellent as part of a Thanksgiving dinner bread basket. Maple Pecan Butter *also translates well to mixing with mashed sweet potatoes for dinner; it's good on waffles or pancakes too. Butter gives muffins a distinctive rich flavor, but oil gives them better "keeping power." Take your pick.*

PUMPKIN MUFFINS

- 2 **cups all-purpose flour**
- 2 **teaspoons baking powder**
- 2 **teaspoons pumpkin pie spice**
- ½ **teaspoon baking soda**
- ¼ **teaspoon salt**
- 1 **egg**
- ⅔ **cup packed light brown sugar**
- ¾ **cup well-shaken buttermilk**
- ¾ **cup canned pumpkin**
- 7 **tablespoons butter, melted or vegetable oil**
- 3 **tablespoons maple syrup**

MAPLE PECAN BUTTER

- ¼ **cup finely chopped toasted pecans**
- ½ **cup softened butter**
- 2 **tablespoons maple syrup**

● Heat oven to 375°F. Grease bottoms only of 12 standard-size muffin cups or line with paper liners.

● In mixing bowl, whisk together flour, baking powder, pumpkin pie spice, baking soda and salt. In another mixing bowl, whisk egg to blend; whisk in brown sugar, breaking up any lumps. Whisk in buttermilk, pumpkin, melted butter and 3 tablespoons maple syrup until smooth. Add dry ingredients; mix with spoon until all ingredients are moistened. Batter may have small lumps; do not overmix.

● Divide batter among muffin cups, filling each about three-fourths full. Bake until muffins are well risen, golden brown and tops are firm, 20 to 23 minutes. Transfer to wire rack to cool slightly. (These muffins are best on baking day, but can be made up to 1 month ahead and frozen, especially if made with oil.) Serve warm with *Maple Pecan Butter.*

● While muffins are baking, prepare *Maple Pecan Butter.* In small bowl, use spatula or whisk to blend pecans, softened butter and 2 tablespoons maple syrup until light and fluffy. Use immediately or refrigerate up to 12 hours. Return to room temperature before using.

12 muffins.

Preparation time: 25 minutes.
Ready to serve: 50 minutes.

SPICED WARM APPLE COMPOTE

If you substitute apple brandy for half of the cider and serve the compote topped with a scoop of rich vanilla or butter-pecan ice cream, you have a dessert worthy of Thanksgiving dinner. It's apple pie without the crust, but with the à la mode!

1 **cinnamon stick, broken in half**
6 **allspice berries**
6 **whole cloves**
2 **lb. tart apples, peeled, thickly sliced**
1 **cup good-quality apple cider**
½ **cup packed dark brown sugar**
2 **tablespoons butter**

● Tie cinnamon stick, allspice and cloves in cheesecloth. In deep skillet or saucepan with lid, combine apples, cider, brown sugar and butter; add spice bag. Bring mixture to a simmer over medium heat, stirring to dissolve sugar and melt butter. Cover; reduce heat to medium-low. Simmer, stirring occasionally, until apples are just tender, about 10 minutes. Uncover; simmer, stirring occasionally and taking care not to mash apples much, until liquid is reduced to a light syrup, about 10 minutes. Remove spice bag. Serve immediately or let cool and refrigerate up to 12 hours. Warm gently in skillet or microwave oven before serving.

4 servings (3½ cups apples, with ¾ cup syrup).

Preparation time: 30 minutes.
Ready to serve: 50 minutes.

*D*ecorated Note Cards

It's sometimes easy to forget exactly why we're celebrating certain holidays. Here's a simple but meaningful way to make sure Thanksgiving doesn't go without thanks. Distribute these decorated blank note cards at breakfast, one to each member of the celebration, and ask each person to write what they are thankful for inside, preferably in private. Designate a basket or box for their return and then, at the traditional Thanksgiving feast later, have one person read the cards. Guests can try and guess who wrote each one; whoever guesses right might even win a prize.

MATERIALS

- **Blank greeting cards and matching envelopes**
- **Multicolored construction paper**
- **Craft glue**

INSTRUCTIONS

1. Choose a Thanksgiving image, such as the pilgrim shown in the photo at left. Cut appropriate colored pieces of construction paper into the desired shapes and glue  onto the outside of the greeting card. Make one card for each member of the celebration. Other image ideas include a turkey, a ship (The Mayflower) or an autumn leaf.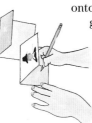

Fun and Easy Thanksgiving

by Cort Sinnes

Do you want to have the best turkey you've ever eaten this Thanksgiving? Do you want to sleep in Thanksgiving morning instead of getting up at 6 a.m. to put the turkey in the oven? All you need to accomplish this seemingly magical feat is a covered kettle grill, a 10-lb. bag of charcoal and the turkey.

I've cooked at least a hundred turkeys this way—so many that I finally gave the process a name—Pandora's Turkey—which refers to the fact that you don't, under any circumstances, take the lid off the grill until the fire goes out. Pandora's Turkey turns beautifully brown and crisp on the outside, moist on the inside (just the way you've always wanted it). The extraordinary part of this procedure is that once I discovered it, I've never had a turkey take more than three hours to cook. So don't tell Aunt Hattie that the turkey took only three hours to cook until after she's taken her first bite and pronounced it the moistest, most delicious turkey she's ever tasted.

Of course, turkey (even great turkey) by itself is no fun, so I've included wonderful accompaniments too.

MENU

Pandora's Turkey

Roasted Beets and Carrots with Orange-Ginger Sauce

Fresh Cranberry and Tangerine Relish

Steamed Persimmon Pudding with Hard Sauce

Succotash

CRAFT

Creative Thanksgiving Placemats

PANDORA'S TURKEY

If it seems like the procedure given here is overly long, it's only because I've tried to answer all the questions that have come up over the years. There seems to be something about cooking the main course for a holiday meal that causes a normally confident cook to become cautious. Rest assured, this is the easiest possible way to cook a turkey. Read the step tips below before you get started.

Covered, kettle-type grill (recipe will not work on any other type of grill)

10 lb. **premium brand charcoal briquettes (not natural, lump charcoal)**

1 **(18- to 22-lb.) turkey (larger if it will fit on your grill, covered)**

1 **disposable aluminum roasting pan, just big enough to fit the turkey**

2 **onions, coarsely chopped**

5 **ribs celery, coarsely chopped**

2 **tablespoons poultry seasoning or dried sage**

A few metal or bamboo skewers

½ **cup vegetable oil**

Salt and freshly ground pepper

● Start with clean grill, free of old coals and ash. Ignite 5 lb. briquettes. (Five lb. may seem like a lot, but this is a special procedure.)

● While waiting for coals to light, prepare turkey for stuffing. Remove neck and giblets from inside of bird; reserve for making gravy, if desired. Wash bird thoroughly with cold water; pat dry with towel, absorbing as much moisture—both inside and out—as possible. Place turkey in aluminum roasting pan.

● In large bowl, mix together onions, celery and poultry seasoning. Place handful of mixture inside neck cavity of turkey. Pull skin over cavity; thread closed using small skewer. Put remaining mixture in body cavity; fasten closed with another skewer. Secure legs to tail using metal fastener found on most store-bought turkeys. Rub entire surface of turkey with oil. Sprinkle liberally with salt (use seasoned salt, if desired) and pepper.

● Check the fire. Coals are just right when completely covered with fine, gray ash. Once at that stage (usually 20 to 25 minutes after lighting), push to either side of grate in equal quantities, leaving center open. Put cooking grid in place. Position roasting pan and turkey in center of grill; cover with lid, leaving top and bottom vents completely open.

● The turkey is done when coals have burned out, usually 2½ hours. (You can tell the coals have burned out when turkey no longer makes cooking noises and smoke stops coming out of vents.) Remove lid—and voilà! A beautifully roasted, mahogany-brown, crisp-on-the-outside, moist-on-the-inside turkey. Carefully transfer bird from roasting pan to carving board; let rest 20 to 30 minutes, loosely tented with foil. (This allows juices to return to interior of meat, making turkey much easier to carve.) Add any juices that accumulate on carving board to your gravy, or use for moistening stuffing.

18-22 servings.

Preparation time: 40 minutes.
Ready to serve: 4½ hours.

Notes on Pandora's Turkey

• Look for a bird that is as squat as possible; a high breastbone prevents grill lid from closing completely. Over the years, I've found that turkeys weighing 18 to 22 lb. fit best. If you want a larger bird, do a test before you unwrap the bird. Simply place turkey on grill (unlit, of course) and make sure lid closes completely. (For birds larger than 22 lb., ignite an extra lb. of charcoal and add 30 minutes to cooking time.)

• I roast turkeys with an aromatic stuffing, one not meant for eating, as outlined in the recipe. If you choose this route and plan on making broth from the turkey carcass afterward, hang on to the aromatic stuffing. It improves the flavor of the broth.

• There will be plenty of juices in roasting pan. These can be divided between flavoring gravy and moistening overcooked stuffing. So far there have been no complaints in the stuffing department. In fact, no one has ever detected that it was cooked outside the bird.

• Turkeys cooked in covered kettle grills don't need basting. In fact, if you remove the lid to baste (or even just to peek), you'll blow the whole process. The rapid influx of air causes coals to heat up quickly, resulting in an uneven cooking temperature and shortened life of the coals. At least that's the only explanation I've ever been able to come up with that makes any sense. At any rate, leave the lid on the grill until the fire goes out. You know what happened to Pandora . . .

ROASTED BEETS AND CARROTS WITH ORANGE-GINGER SAUCE

In the days of the Pilgrims, beets and carrots were of the mammoth variety—the best size for winter keeping—and were traditionally roasted over or in the coals. Once you've tried them, you'll wonder why we ever stopped cooking them that way. Absolutely delicious!

The largest beets and carrots you can find (as many as you care to cook)

ORANGE-GINGER SAUCE
  2 tablespoons mayonnaise
 ¼ cup fresh orange juice
 ¼ teaspoon salt
 ½ cup grated unpeeled fresh ginger
   Finely chopped fresh parsley, for garnish (optional)

● To charcoal-roast beets: After removing tops, either lay beets directly on top of white-hot charcoal briquettes or, if you have enough briquettes, bury beets in hot coals. Cook 45 to 60 minutes, depending on size (hardball-size beets roast tender in about 45 minutes). If beets rest on top of coals, turn once or twice to evenly char on all sides. Once beets are tender, remove from coals to cool for easy handling. Using sharp knife, remove charred skins; slice beets ⅜ inch thick.

● To charcoal-roast carrots: Wash and scrub (but don't peel) carrots; place on cooking grate directly over white-hot coals. Turn every 10 to 12 minutes until nicely browned on all sides. Large carrots cook tender in 35 to 45 minutes. Allow to cool slightly; slice lengthwise ⅜ inch thick.

● To prepare sauce: In bowl, combine mayonnaise, orange juice and salt. Using your hands, gather grated ginger together in a ball; squeeze tightly over mayonnaise mixture. (You'll be amazed at the amount of juice that comes out.) Discard pulp. Stir sauce. Arrange warm beets and carrots on platter; drizzle with sauce. Garnish with parsley, if using.

Vegetables as desired, with ½ cup sauce.

Preparation time: 30 minutes.
Ready to serve: 2 hours.

Fresh Cranberry and Tangerine Relish

This recipe makes for a refreshing and unusual flavor combination, just right for serving with the charcoal-roasted turkey. Please note that the relish requires two days refrigeration to mellow the pungency of the fresh tangerine rind.

3   **tangerines, unpeeled**
1   **(12-oz.) pkg. fresh cranberries**
1   **cup sugar**
¼   **teaspoon salt**

● Halve tangerines; remove seeds. In food processor, pulse half of the cranberries and half of the tangerines until finely chopped but not pureed. Place mixture in container with tight-fitting lid. Repeat with remaining cranberries and tangerines; stir in sugar and salt. Cover; refrigerate 2 days or up to 2 weeks.

4½ cups.

Preparation time: 10 minutes.
Ready to serve: 10 minutes, plus 2-day chill time.

STEAMED PERSIMMON PUDDING WITH HARD SAUCE

Once you've made this old-fashioned dessert, you may find that you've created a new tradition for your Thanksgiving celebration. Its flavor and texture are a delight and somehow just right for an autumn meal. Steamed pudding molds are readily available at cookware shops. A small scoop of vanilla ice cream is an excellent substitute for the more traditional hard sauce.

1 cup peeled, finely chopped persimmons (about 2 medium)
2 teaspoons baking soda
1 cup all-purpose flour
1 cup sugar
½ teaspoon baking powder
½ teaspoon salt
½ teaspoon ground cinnamon
½ cup milk
1 egg, beaten
1 cup chopped walnuts
1 tablespoon butter, melted
½ teaspoon vanilla

● In small bowl, combine persimmons and baking soda; let stand a few minutes.

● Meanwhile, in separate bowl, sift together flour, sugar, baking powder, salt and cinnamon.

● Gradually add milk and egg to persimmons, which will have jelled. Add persimmon mixture to flour mixture; stir well. Stir in walnuts, butter and vanilla. Pour batter into greased 1- to 1½-quart pudding mold with lid; steam on rack in Dutch oven with simmering water 1½ to 2 hours or until knife inserted in center of pudding comes out clean. Do not boil dry. (Can also steam in top of pasta cooker with removable insert.) Cool slightly; remove from rack. Serve warm or at room temperature with *Hard Sauce.*

Hard Sauce

¾ **cup sugar**
1 **tablespoon cornstarch**
  Dash salt
1 **cup water**
1 **egg, beaten**
1 **tablespoon butter**
1 **teaspoon vanilla**
1 **oz. brandy**

● In medium saucepan, blend sugar, cornstarch, salt and water. Cook and stir until bubbly. Place egg in small bowl; stir in a small amount of hot mixture. Slowly add egg mixture to saucepan; cook over medium heat, stirring constantly, until sauce thickens. Add butter, vanilla and brandy; stir well. Serve hot over slices of *Steamed Persimmon Pudding*.

8 servings, with 1¾ cups sauce.

Preparation time: 45 minutes.
Ready to serve: 2 hours.

SUCCOTASH

This is a particularly flavorful variation of a Native American dish that traditionally combines lima beans and corn. If someone in your group just can't abide limas, replace the beans with red kidney beans or fava beans.

2 cups frozen or fresh baby lima beans
2 tablespoons butter
1 medium onion, diced
½ red bell pepper, diced
2 cups fresh or frozen corn kernels
½ cup heavy cream
½ teaspoon dried thyme
   Salt and freshly ground pepper to taste
   Hot pepper sauce to taste
2 tablespoons fresh parsley, finely chopped (optional)

● Cook lima beans according to package directions or, if using fresh limas, place in saucepan with enough salted water to cover. Bring to a boil; reduce heat to medium. Cook until just tender, 12 to 15 minutes; drain.

● In large skillet, melt butter over medium heat. Sauté onion and bell pepper until soft. Add lima beans and corn; mix well. Add cream, thyme, salt, pepper and hot pepper sauce; heat until bubbling. Continue cooking 3 to 5 minutes or until sauce is thickened and vegetables are tender. Place succotash in serving dish; sprinkle with parsley, if using.

4 cups.

Preparation time: 35 minutes.
Ready to serve: 35 minutes.

Creative Thanksgiving Placemats

*I*t's great for kids to have a creative project to participate in, especially during holiday meal preparation time. These laminated placemats are not only easy to assemble, they make great keepsakes from one Thanksgiving to the next. Be sure to have everyone sign and date his or her creations so the occasion can be remembered.

MATERIALS

- **Lamination sheets, at least 9 by 12 inches (available at stationery and craft stores)**
- **Plain white drawing paper, cut into 8- by 11-inch rectangles**
- **Pencil**
- **Colored construction paper**
- **X-acto knife or scissors**
- **Craft glue or spray adhesive**
- **Colored felt-tipped pens**

INSTRUCTIONS

1. Provide each person with a sheet of white drawing paper, 8 by 11 inches.

2. Have each person trace his or her hand onto a piece of construction paper. Glue the hand-shape onto the center of the drawing paper. Let each person use their creativity to make the hand-shape into a turkey. Sign and date the artwork using felt-tipped pens.

3. Peel the backing from two lamination sheets. Press one on the top, flip over, and place one on the back, lining up the edges. Use the palm of your hand to smooth out any air bubbles.

Hanukkah Lite

by Bruce Weinstein

Traditional Jewish cooking rarely skimps on fat, and never on taste. Staying within the bounds of kosher law (no shellfish, pork or meat mixed with dairy), a festive dinner can include anything from stuffed breast of veal to honey cake. But certain dishes must be prepared on specific occasions. During the eight days of Hanukkah, the festival of lights, we always indulge in potato latkes (fried potato pancakes). These time-honored savories hold court as we light the candles, exchange presents and spin the dreidel. Even at a "lite" Hanukkah meal, potato latkes have their place, turning out just as crisp and tender in the oven as they do in a skillet of hot oil. But baked latkes are only part of this calorie-conscious celebration. All of these recipes are light on fat, but in true Jewish tradition are anything but light on flavor. So grate the potatoes, kiss your bubbe and dance with the rabbi. When he asks why you're so light on your feet, tell him it's the food.

MENU

Tsimmes Soup

Baked Potato Latkes

Veal and Mushroom Loaves

Warm Apple Chutney

Lemon Sorbet with Mixed Berries and Vodka

CRAFT

Handmade Candle Box

TSIMMES SOUP

Tsimmes, that rich combination of sweet potatoes, carrots, prunes and honey, is served at many Jewish holidays to represent how sweet life is. This version forgoes the prunes, but offers golden raisins, another sweet bounty—one that helps this soup maintain its bright orange color.

6 **cups reduced-sodium chicken broth**
1 **lb. carrots, cut into ½-inch rounds**
1 **large sweet potato* (about ¾ lb.),
   peeled, cut into 1-inch dice**
¾ **cup golden raisins**
1 **(4-inch) cinnamon stick**
3 **tablespoons honey**
1 **tablespoon lemon juice**
½ **teaspoon salt**
½ **teaspoon freshly ground white pepper**
¼ **teaspoon grated nutmeg****
2 **tablespoons chopped fresh chives**

● In large pot, bring broth, carrots, sweet potato, raisins and cinnamon stick to a boil over high heat. Reduce heat to medium; simmer partially covered 30 minutes or until vegetables can be mashed with back of spoon. Remove and discard cinnamon stick.

● With slotted spoon, remove vegetables to blender or food processor; add ½ cup hot liquid. Puree until smooth. Return puree to pot over low heat. Whisk in honey, lemon juice, salt, pepper and nutmeg; heat 10 minutes. Sprinkle with chives.

TIPS *Look for deep orange-colored sweet potatoes, often labeled "yams."

**To grate whole nutmeg, use a nutmeg grater—a small metal grater with fine holes— or use the fine holes on a cheese grater.

6 (1-cup) servings.

Preparation time: 20 minutes.
Ready to serve: 1 hour.

Baked Potato Latkes

These baked potato pancakes are the stuff of calorie counters' dreams—crisp, rich and made with only a fraction of the oil usually required to fry latkes. Muffin tins help keep the latkes uniform and nonstick cooking spray makes the tops extra crunchy.

2½ lb. Yukon Gold potatoes
 1 large onion
 ¼ cup vegetable oil
 2 eggs, lightly beaten
 ¼ cup matzo meal
 2 teaspoons salt
 ½ teaspoon freshly ground pepper

● Heat oven to 400°F. Generously spray 12 muffin cups (preferably nonstick) with nonstick cooking spray.

● Peel and shred potatoes using food processor or large holes of box grater. Squeeze out extra moisture with your hands; place potatoes in large bowl. Shred onion into potatoes.

● Add oil, eggs, matzo meal, salt and pepper to potatoes; stir until well combined. Divide among muffin cups (about ⅓ cup each); press down lightly to compact mixture. Bake 40 minutes; remove from oven. Spray tops with nonstick cooking spray. Bake 20 minutes more or until crisp and brown.

6 servings.

Preparation time: 25 minutes.
Ready to serve: 1 hour, 25 minutes.

VEAL AND MUSHROOM LOAVES

For the lightest meat loaves, grind your own veal or ask your butcher to do it for you. Choose a lean cut and trim as much exterior fat as possible. The delicate taste of the veal allows the flavor of the mushrooms to come through, so use brown mushrooms if you can find them; they have a nuttier taste.

3	**tablespoons olive oil**
1	**rib celery, minced**
1	**small onion, minced**
1	**lb. crimini mushrooms or other brown mushrooms, finely minced***
1½	**lb. ground veal**
½	**cup dry bread crumbs**
1	**egg**
2	**tablespoons tomato paste**
1	**tablespoon Worcestershire sauce**
1	**teaspoon dried thyme**
½	**teaspoon salt**
½	**teaspoon freshly ground pepper**

● Heat large sauté pan over medium heat until hot. Add 2 tablespoons of the oil; swirl to coat bottom of pan. Add celery and onion; cook 3 to 5 minutes or until soft and lightly brown, stirring often. Add remaining tablespoon oil and mushrooms to pan; cook, stirring often, 5 to 7 minutes or until mushrooms give off all their liquid and mixture is nearly dry. Transfer mixture to large bowl to cool.

● Heat oven to 350°F. Add veal, bread crumbs, egg, tomato paste, Worcestershire, thyme, salt and pepper to cooled vegetables; mix until well combined. Divide mixture into 6 equal parts, about ¾ cup each; shape each into small, flattened oval. Place in large roasting pan at least 1½ inches apart. Bake 30 minutes or until golden brown and no longer pink in center. Serve with *Warm Apple Chutney* (page 117).

TIP *To finely mince mushrooms, pulse them in a food processor, stopping just before they look pureed.

6 servings.

Preparation time: 30 minutes.
Ready to serve: 1 hour, 5 minutes.

WARM APPLE CHUTNEY

Macintosh apples are often used in cooking for their crisp texture. Plus their tartness balances added sugar without creating a dessert. Since this sweet and salty condiment is cooked briefly, Macintosh are the perfect choice. They soften slightly, creating a smooth yet chunky condiment.

2 tablespoons vegetable oil
1 large onion, thinly sliced
1 red bell pepper, diced
1 garlic clove, minced
4 medium Macintosh apples, peeled, cored and thinly sliced*
2 tablespoons water
¼ cup packed light brown sugar
2 tablespoons Worcestershire sauce

● In large sauté pan, heat oil over medium-high heat. Add onion, bell pepper and garlic; cook, stirring often, 3 to 5 minutes or until onion is soft and translucent.

● Add apples to pan; cook 3 minutes or until apples begin to soften. Add water and brown sugar; cook about 2 minutes or until sugar is dissolved and apples break down slightly. Add Worcestershire; cook 2 minutes or until mixture is bubbling and slightly thickened. Remove from heat. Cover; keep warm before serving over *Veal and Mushroom Loaves* (page 116).

TIP *Place peeled apples in water with a small amount of vinegar added to it until ready to sauté; this keeps them from turning brown.

3¼ cups.

Preparation time: 30 minutes.
Ready to serve: 30 minutes.

LEMON SORBET WITH MIXED BERRIES AND VODKA

Not only does this dessert explode with flavor, it's easy to make and 100% fat-free. Even though there are only three tablespoons of vodka in this recipe, you may not want to serve it to your kids. Buy an extra container of berries to top their sorbet, keeping it zero-proof.

- **6 large strawberries, stems removed, cut into eighths**
- **½ pint raspberries**
- **½ pint blueberries**
- **3 tablespoons currant-flavored vodka***
- **2 tablespoons sugar**
- **1 teaspoon finely grated lemon peel**
- **1 quart lemon sorbet**

● In large bowl, toss strawberries, raspberries, blueberries, vodka, sugar and lemon peel until well combined. Cover; refrigerate 3 hours or up to 3 days.

● Divide sorbet among 6 serving bowls; top each with ⅓ cup berry mixture.

TIP *Vanilla, cinnamon or plain vodka also work well with berries.

6 servings.

Preparation time: 10 minutes.
Ready to serve: 3 hours, 10 minutes.

Handmade Candle Box

A handmade box, specially created for holding candles for the menorah, only increases the importance of the ceremony. Smoke shops routinely give away (or charge a very small price for) empty cigar boxes, just the thing for this craft. It's a good idea to buy your candles first to make sure you procure the right size box!

MATERIALS

- Cigar box, large enough to fit menorah candles
- Metallic gold paper
- X-acto knife
- Ornate wrapping paper
- Small piece of foamcore
- Black felt-tipped pen
- Pencil
- Blue construction paper
- Spray adhesive

INSTRUCTIONS

1. Measure each external side of the cigar box. Cut a separate sheet of metallic paper for each individual side, approximately ½ inch wider on all sides.

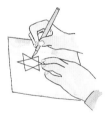

2. Spray the underside of each cut piece of paper with spray adhesive. Press into place, smoothing out air bubbles. Trim overage with the X-acto knife.

3. Repeat steps 1 and 2 for the inside of the cigar box, using the ornate wrapping paper.

4. Using the X-acto knife, cut out a Star of David shape. Cut a square of the metallic paper, slightly larger than the Star of David. Spray the underside of the paper with spray adhesive and press onto the foamcore. Trim excess, using the X-acto knife. Blacken sides of the star with the felt-tipped pen.

5. Using a pencil, trace the Star of David onto the blue construction paper. Using the X-acto knife, cut the shape approximately ¼ inch larger than the tracing. Glue the blue construction paper onto the bottom of the Star of David and then glue the whole thing onto the top of the box.

6. Store candles in the box—a much more festive and meaningful place than a package from the store.

Christmas Eve Family Dinner

by Carole Brown

Christmas need not be formal to be meaningful or memorable. In fact, simple family celebrations—with good food and good fun—are the stuff that the fondest memories are made of. Here's a chance to create such a tradition in your home, with this happy and hearty menu for a hungry family. From Sparkling Party Punch *to* Hot Pot Roast Sandwiches, Roasted Sweet and White Potatoes with Rosemary, *and* Pumpkin Custard, *this Christmas Eve dinner is a very special one.*

MENU

Sparkling Party Punch

Goat Cheese Christmas Hors d'Oeuvre

Hot Pot Roast Sandwiches

Roasted Sweet and White Potatoes with Rosemary

Pumpkin Custard

CRAFT

Decorative Paper Masks

SPARKLING PARTY PUNCH

Make this fruit punch with ginger ale or sparkling wine, or divide it in half and make one pitcher of nonalcoholic punch and the other with wine. If you use frozen juice concentrate, use slightly less water than the can's instructions call for; for example, if the can says to mix the concentrate with 3 cans water, use 2½ cans. This gives you more flavorful juice for your punch base. If you wish, garnish the punch with whole or sliced strawberries, red grapes, orange slices, raspberries or fresh mint sprigs.

2½ **cups cranberry juice, chilled**
2½ **cups orange juice, chilled**
2½ **cups limeade or lemonade, chilled**
 1 **quart ginger ale, chilled or 1 bottle chilled sparkling wine**
   Cut-up fresh fruit (optional)

● In 1-gallon container, mix cranberry juice, orange juice and limeade.

● Just before serving, stir in ginger ale or sparkling wine. Garnish with fruit as desired.

14 to 16 servings (11½ cups.).

Preparation time: 10 minutes.
Ready to serve: 10 minutes.

VARIATION Stir ¾ cup crème de cassis, Grand Marnier or other liqueur into the sparkling wine punch.

NOTE To make both kinds of punch, divide juice base between 2 containers. Stir 2 cups ginger ale into half of the juice and 1½ to 2 cups sparkling wine into the other half. This makes 7 to 8 servings of each.

GOAT CHEESE CHRISTMAS HORS D'OEUVRE

Prepare these colorful hors d'oeuvres several hours in advance; the flavors will mellow and the dried spices will soften. Choose a fresh (not aged) moist goat cheese that will easily roll into balls. We've made red, green and white cheese bites for Christmas colors. You can substitute other favorite spices such as curry powder or black pepper.

1 **(5- to 6-oz.) pkg. fresh goat cheese***

1 to 2 **tablespoons paprika or chili powder**

1 to 2 **tablespoons finely minced fresh herbs, such as dill, chives, parsley or a combination**

● Divide cheese into 16 to 20 pieces; roll into small balls. If cheese gets sticky, chill a few minutes.

● Put paprika and herbs in separate bowls. Roll one-third of cheese balls in each seasoning, leaving one-third of the balls white. Spear each ball with decorative toothpick; arrange on platter. Loosely cover; chill until ready to serve.

TIP *Cream cheese can be used instead of the goat cheese; 1 (3-oz.) pkg. makes about 16 balls.

16 to 20 hors d'oeuvres.

Preparation time: 10 minutes.
Ready to serve: 40 minutes.

HOT POT ROAST SANDWICHES

These warm and hearty beef sandwiches are ideal for any family gathering. Make the easy beef-and-onion pot roast a day ahead; make the delicious quick "gravy" by pureeing the pot roast broth and onions. Serve meat and sauce poor-boy style in large rolls, or open-face atop bread slices.

3 to 3½ **lb. boneless beef chuck roast (about 1½ inches thick)**
    1 **teaspoon salt, plus more to taste**
    ¼ **teaspoon freshly ground pepper, plus more to taste**
    2 **tablespoons canola or other vegetable oil, plus more if needed**
    4 **cups sliced onions**
    1 **teaspoon dried thyme**
    1 **cup reduced-sodium chicken, beef or vegetable broth, plus ½ to 1 cup more if needed**
    1 **tablespoon tomato paste**
2 to 3 **teaspoons Worcestershire sauce**
    8 **sandwich rolls or bread slices**

● Heat oven to 325°F. Trim excess fat from beef; pat beef dry with paper towels. Mix 1 teaspoon salt and ¼ teaspoon pepper; rub lightly onto surface of beef. Heat Dutch oven (or other stew pot with tight-fitting lid) over medium-high heat; add 2 tablespoons oil. Brown beef, about 4 minutes per side. Remove beef; hold on plate.

● Add onions, thyme and another drizzle of oil if needed to Dutch oven. Toss and lightly brown onions; add broth and tomato paste. Scrape up brown bits from bottom of pan. Set beef on top of onions; bring to a simmer. Cover with foil and lid; put pot in oven. Check pot after 30 minutes. Liquid should be at slow simmer; adjust oven temperature if necessary.

● Bake until beef is fork-tender and onions are completely soft, 2 to 2½ hours total oven time. Turn meat once about halfway through baking time. Remove meat to plate; tent loosely with foil to prevent drying. Strain onions from

broth. Cool and refrigerate beef, broth and onions in separate containers.

● The next day (or after several hours), remove congealed fat from top of broth. You should have 2½ to 3 cups broth; add more if needed. Return onions to broth; puree in food processor or blender to make thick sauce.

● With large fork, slice meat thinly against grain or shred into bite-size pieces. To serve, place sauce and beef in saucepan. Season to taste with Worcestershire, salt and pepper. Heat beef and sauce. Serve in rolls or on bread slices.

8 sandwiches.

Preparation time: 40 minutes.
Ready to serve: 3 hours, 15 minutes.

Roasted Sweet and White Potatoes with Rosemary

These versatile and simple potatoes seem to be very popular with young people. The potatoes are delicious anytime—with roast chicken dinner or as finger food with burgers. They're usually made with regular baking potatoes, but we like to mix them with sweet potatoes for the holidays.

2   **medium to large baking potatoes, scrubbed, patted dry**

2   **sweet potatoes, about same size as baking potatoes, scrubbed, patted dry**

3 to 4   **tablespoons olive oil**

2   **teaspoons finely chopped fresh rosemary**

1   **teaspoon dried thyme**

¼   **teaspoon salt**
    Generous dash freshly ground pepper

● Heat oven to 400°F. Cut each potato into 8 or more lengthwise slices.

● In bowl, mix oil, rosemary, thyme, salt and pepper; toss with potatoes. Spread potatoes on baking sheet; bake about 45 minutes or until soft and lightly browned. Turn potatoes once with tongs if necessary for even browning.

8 servings.

Preparation time: 10 minutes.
Ready to serve: 55 minutes.

PUMPKIN CUSTARD

This silky custard, dusted with crushed gingersnaps, gives you all the flavor of pumpkin pie without having to make a crust. It's served chilled, so make it a day or several hours ahead. Serve at the table or on a buffet.

1 **cup sugar**
½ **teaspoon salt**
1½ **teaspoons ground ginger**
1½ **teaspoons ground cinnamon**
1½ **teaspoons ground allspice**
½ **teaspoon freshly grated nutmeg**
3 **eggs**
3 **egg yolks**
2 **(15-oz.) cans or 1 (29-oz.) can pumpkin (about 3½ cups)**
1½ **teaspoons vanilla**
2½ **cups whole milk**

GARNISH
1½ **cups whipping cream**
2 **tablespoons sugar**
½ to ¾ **cup crushed gingersnap cookies**

● Put rack in center of oven; heat oven to 350°F. In small bowl, mix 1 cup sugar, salt, ginger, cinnamon, allspice and nutmeg.

● In large mixing bowl, whisk eggs and egg yolks to combine well. Stir in pumpkin and vanilla. Sift sugar mixture over pumpkin; stir to combine. Stir in milk.

● Place 12 (6-oz.) glass custard cups* in low-sided roasting pan; divide custard evenly among cups. Put pan on oven rack; make water bath (pour in hot tap water until it comes halfway up sides of cups)*. Bake 40 to 45 minutes or until custards are slightly puffed and toothpick comes out clean. Remove cups from water bath to cool. Cover; refrigerate until ready to serve.

● In mixing bowl, whip cream and 2 tablespoons sugar. Top custards with whipped cream; sprinkle with crushed gingersnaps. Store in refrigerator.

TIPS *Instead of baking custard in custard cups, you can use a 2-quart (13x9-inch) gratin pan. Bake in water bath as directed; larger pan should bake 50 to 60 minutes.

**To bake custard without a water bath, reduce oven temperature to 325°F. Custard will be slightly less silky in texture and a little drier.

12 servings.

Preparation time: 30 minutes.
Ready to serve: 3 hours, 10 minutes.

Decorative Paper Masks

A Christmas Eve dinner can be as formal or fun as your family desires. In some households, Christmas Eve is the time to exchange just one special gift as part of the evening's celebration. These masks can serve double duty: as table decorations and as a way to disguise the identity of Christmas Eve gift-givers. As simple as they are, they dramatically change the way a person looks, usually with laughter-producing results. Keep a camera handy!

MATERIALS

- Mat board, approximately 4 by 7 inches for each mask
- Pair of eyeglasses
- Pencil
- Tracing paper
- Multicolored construction paper
- X-acto knife
- ¼-inch-diameter wooden dowels, approximately 12 inches long
- Craft glue
- Hot glue gun

INSTRUCTIONS

1. Using an X-acto knife, cut the mat board into approximately 4- by 7-inch rectangles.

2. Position the eyeglasses in the middle of the mat board and, using a pencil, trace around the outside of them. On the tracing, mark the center of each "lens" approximately where you would look through the glasses.

3. Using the X-acto knife, cut two ½-inch-diameter holes where your eyes will look through the mask. Trim the sides of the mat board into a mask shape, as shown in the illustration.

4. Make a drawing of the mask on a piece of tracing paper.

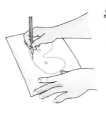

5. Place the tracing paper over the top of the construction paper. Using an X-acto knife, cut through the tracing paper and all the way through the construction paper, using the tracing paper as you would a dressmaker's pattern.

6. Glue the different pieces of construction paper together to create the mask. Allow to dry and then glue the mask to the mat board,

making sure the eye-holes are in the correct position. Using the X-acto knife, cut eye-holes in the mask so they match up with the eye-holes in the mat board.

7. Using hot glue, affix the wooden dowel to the mat board.

Cozy Christmas Eve Dinner

by Mark Scarbrough

Christmas Eve is a special time that deserves special food. So come in from the cold to this hearty menu, designed for a relaxing evening with family or friends. Start with a cup of cheer, then move on to a bright, light starter, a welcome taste of sunnier times ahead. Come back to the deep season with a hearty but exotic soup, so flavor-packed it cries out for crusty bread—this one, a new take on an Irish favorite. Finish the evening with a dessert made to commemorate that time of year when winter comes full on—when the nights are long, the wind sharp and family and friends near.

    You can prepare all these dishes earlier in the day, so your evening is, well, yours. Nothing here is heavy—because an evening of conversation and Christmas dinner tomorrow still lie ahead. But it's all comfort food, the antidote to the chill, the celebration of the season.

MENU

Hot Cider Punch

Cucumber Prosciutto Rolls

Curried Squash and Chestnut Soup with Wild Mushrooms

Herb Buttermilk Soda Bread

Dried Fruit Compote

CRAFT

Fragrant Pineapple Urn Centerpiece

HOT CIDER PUNCH

This Christmas warmer is a delicious start to an evening at home, ready right when company arrives. The bay leaf may be a surprise, but it adds a savory hint to the cider, a "back taste" in culinary terms. The accompanying "rimmer" is a simple combination of nuts and sugar, a good way to dress up this treat—"pearls under the shawl," as they say in the South. The liquor is optional, of course. You can also substitute vodka for bourbon, if you prefer a more subtle taste.

RIMMER

¼ cup slivered almonds
3 tablespoons sugar
½ teaspoon ground cinnamon

PUNCH

6 cups apple juice or cider
2 teaspoons sugar
2-inch piece fresh ginger, peeled
1 orange, cut into quarters
8 allspice berries
5 whole cloves
1 bay leaf
¼ teaspoon salt
6 oz. bourbon (optional)
3 oz. cinnamon schnapps (optional)

● For Rimmer: Heat oven to 375°F. Place almonds on large baking sheet; toast 4 to 6 minutes or until golden, stirring once. Cool completely; place almonds, 3 tablespoons sugar and cinnamon in food processor. Pulse until finely ground, scraping down bowl as needed. Spread on large plate; set aside.

● For Punch: In large saucepan, combine apple juice, 2 teaspoons sugar, ginger, orange, allspice, cloves, bay leaf and salt over medium heat. Cover; simmer 15 minutes.

● To serve, dip rims of 6 mugs in hot cider, then dip in rimmer. If using, pour 1 oz. bourbon and ½ oz. schnapps in each mug. Strain cider into mugs.

6 cups punch, with ½ cup rimmer.

Preparation time: 10 minutes.
Ready to serve: 25 minutes.

CUCUMBER PROSCIUTTO ROLLS

At first blush, this starter seems too much like springtime. It can't be Christmas Eve, can it? (You can always revisit this recipe later in the year.) But Christmas is a time of hope, of light—of which this bright first course reminds us. Chill is in the air, but spring is coming. We can see it from afar. White sesame seeds are available in some gourmet markets and in most health food stores.

½ **cup white sesame seeds**
3 **large cucumbers, preferably seedless, peeled**
3 **oz. thinly sliced prosciutto, cut into 1-inch strips**
1 **cup crème fraîche**
2 **tablespoons rice vinegar**
½ **teaspoon sugar**
½ **teaspoon salt**
2 **teaspoons chopped fresh tarragon**

● Heat oven to 375°F. Spread sesame seeds on baking sheet; toast 2 to 4 minutes or until seeds are golden, stirring once or twice. Spread on large plate.

● Cut ⅛ inch from 1 side of each cucumber to create flat surface. Lay cucumbers cut-side down on work surface. Using vegetable peeler or very sharp knife, make long thin strips of cucumber, beginning at 1 end and pulling steadily to the other. Repeat with all cucumbers, making 18 strips or more if some are narrow.

● Lay 1 cucumber strip on work surface (if strip is narrow, lay 2 together). Top with 2 or 3 strips prosciutto; roll up, then roll in sesame seeds. Repeat with remaining cucumber, prosciutto and sesame seeds.

● To make dressing, in medium bowl, whisk together crème fraîche, vinegar, sugar and salt; stir in tarragon. Pour dressing over cucumber rolls or use as dip.

18 rolls.

Preparation time: 35 minutes.
Ready to serve: 35 minutes.

CURRIED SQUASH AND CHESTNUT SOUP WITH WILD MUSHROOMS

This comforting vegetarian soup—with no dairy, it's even vegan—makes a nice, light Christmas Eve dinner, especially before the feasting to come on Christmas Day. Steamed or cooked chestnuts are available in many gourmet markets; buy them in glass jars, so you can see that they're plump and firm. Curry powder isn't a spice—it's a blend. This one pays tribute to eastern central India.

1	**large acorn squash (about 1½ lb.)**
1	**teaspoon cumin seed**
1	**teaspoon ground ginger**
1	**teaspoon ground turmeric**
¾	**teaspoon ground cinnamon**
½	**teaspoon fenugreek seeds**
½	**teaspoon ground coriander**
¼	**teaspoon celery seed**
⅛	**teaspoon dry mustard**
⅛	**teaspoon cayenne pepper or to taste**
3	**tablespoons unsalted butter**
1	**medium onion, chopped**
2	**garlic cloves, minced**
1	**(15-oz.) jar steamed or whole cooked chestnuts (about 2⅔ cups), drained**
1	**quart vegetable stock**
½	**cup dry vermouth or dry sherry**
1	**lb. wild mushrooms, such as crimini, hedgehog, lobster, porcini or black trumpet, cleaned and halved, or cut into chunks**
2	**teaspoons lemon juice**
1	**teaspoon salt**
½	**teaspoon freshly ground pepper**

● Heat oven to 400°F. Spray large baking sheet with nonstick cooking spray. Cut squash in half lengthwise; scoop out seeds and strings with grapefruit spoon. Place on baking sheet, cut-side down. Bake 35 minutes or until soft; cool on wire rack 20 minutes.

● Meanwhile, in spice grinder, coffee grinder or with mortar and pestle, grind cumin, ginger, turmeric, cinnamon, fenugreek, coriander, celery seed, mustard and cayenne. Set aside.

● In large pot, melt 2 tablespoons of the butter over medium heat. Add onion and garlic; sauté 3 minutes or until soft. Add chestnuts; sauté 2 minutes, stirring frequently. Add stock and vermouth. Cover; simmer 20 minutes or until chestnuts soften.

● Scoop soft flesh from squash; add to pot along with spice mixture. Cover; simmer 15 minutes.

● Meanwhile, in large skillet, melt remaining tablespoon butter over medium heat. Add mushrooms; sauté 5 minutes, stirring constantly, until mushrooms brown, give off some of their liquid and liquid evaporates.

● When chestnuts and squash are tender, remove pot from heat. Puree in batches in food processor or with immersion blender. Return to pot; stir in lemon juice, salt and pepper. Add mushrooms. Heat on low until warmed, about 3 minutes. (Soup can be kept up to 3 days covered in refrigerator. Reheat over low heat 10 minutes or in microwave 4 minutes on high.)

11 cups.

Preparation time: 20 minutes.
Ready to serve: 1 hour, 30 minutes.

HERB BUTTERMILK SODA BREAD

Soda bread is an Irish staple, simple and quick. Here, it's gussied up with rosemary, olives and buttermilk for a richer taste. Sifting the flour is necessary, because it aerates the dough, which doesn't rely on yeast for its rise. The amount of flour can vary widely based on its temperature and the day's humidity. If you store flour in the refrigerator, make sure you let it come to room temperature before making this bread.

5 to 6	**cups all-purpose flour**
2	**teaspoons salt**
1½	**teaspoons baking soda**
½	**teaspoon baking powder**
2	**teaspoons chopped fresh rosemary**
2	**cups buttermilk (regular or low-fat)**
2	**tablespoons vegetable oil**
¼	**cup chopped ripe olives**

● Heat oven to 375°F. Spray baking sheet with nonstick cooking spray.

● In large bowl, sift 5 cups flour, salt, baking soda and baking powder using flour sifter or fine-mesh sieve. Stir in rosemary, buttermilk and oil with wooden spoon just until a loose dough forms.

● Turn dough out onto clean work surface. Sprinkle with olives. Knead 5 minutes, pressing down with heel of one hand and pulling with fingers of the other. Add more flour as needed to keep dough from sticking; dough should be smooth and soft, like a baby's skin. Form round loaf, resembling half of a partially deflated basketball.

● Place loaf on baking sheet. Cut an "X" in top with sharp knife. Bake 20 minutes. Reduce temperature to 325°F; continue baking 40 minutes or until loaf sounds hollow when tapped. Cool completely on wire rack before serving or wrap in kitchen towel and store up to 1 day at room temperature.

8x4½-inch round loaf.

Preparation time: 15 minutes.
Ready to serve: 1 hour, 45 minutes.

DRIED FRUIT COMPOTE

This may be the quintessence of winter desserts: fruits long stored, simmered back to life, spiced and then softened. Make this compote up to three days ahead and store covered in the refrigerator. You may need to thin it with an extra half-cup of apple juice, as the fruits may absorb most of the sauce as they sit. Reheat compote in microwave on high 4 minutes, or in covered saucepan over low heat 7 minutes.

COMPOTE

   3 **cups apple juice**
   1 **cup red wine**
   1 **(2-inch) cinnamon stick**
   2 **tablespoons sugar**
   1 **teaspoon grated lemon peel**
   ¼ **teaspoon grated nutmeg**
   ¼ **teaspoon salt**
   ⅛ **teaspoon ground cloves**
1½ **cups (about 5 oz.) dried apples, chopped**
1¼ **cups dried cranberries**
   1 **cup (about 5 oz.) dried plums (prunes)**
   1 **cup (about 6 oz.) dried apricots, chopped**

SWEETENED CHEESE

   8 **oz. mascarpone cheese, at room temperature**
   1 **teaspoon milk (regular or low-fat)**
   2 **tablespoons honey**
   1 **teaspoon vanilla**

● In large saucepan, combine juice and wine over high heat; stir in cinnamon stick, sugar, lemon peel, nutmeg, salt and cloves; bring to a boil. Stir in dried fruit; cover. Reduce heat to low. Simmer 20 minutes or until fruit is tender. Remove cinnamon stick. Cool at room temperature at least 30 minutes, covered.

● In medium bowl, mash mascarpone and milk with fork until smooth; mix in honey and vanilla. Serve by placing 2 tablespoons (or less) sweetened cheese in middle of each soup bowl. Spoon compote around; serve immediately.

6 cups compote, with 1 cup sweetened cheese.

Preparation time: 10 minutes.
Ready to serve: 1 hour.

Fragrant Pineapple Urn Centerpiece

The pineapple has been a traditional symbol of hospitality for generations ... and a delightful display for the holiday season. Inserting whole cloves into the pineapple not only acts as a preservative, but also results in a highly aromatic decoration. Two clove-studded pineapples, placed atop classical urns, make for an impressive buffet table. If the pineapples will be placed next to the wall, only one side needs to be studded with cloves.

MATERIALS

- **2 similar-sized fresh pineapples, as unripe as possible**
- **2 or 3 (1.25-ounce) jars of whole cloves**
- **2 small urns or other stands for displaying pineapples**
- **Optional: Ribbon for bows at base of pineapples**

INSTRUCTIONS

1. Pour cloves in a small bowl. Using your fingers, push cloves into the spaces between the pineapple's diamond-shaped "eyes."

2. Place pineapple on top of urn and festoon with a ribbon where the pineapple meets the urn.

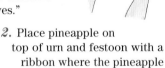

Kids' Christmas Party

by Colleen Miner

Everyone loves receiving gifts. But there is also great joy in giving gifts, especially those we make ourselves. This fun and edible craft party for kids is devoted to making gifts for family, teachers and friends. These gifts are easy to make, delicious to eat and fun to look at. Double batches are probably in order, because much of the gift inventory is sure to disappear at the hands (mouths) of the little creators! Let's get the party started with a Pizza Roll to see if we can minimize the plunder on the sweet creations to come.

MENU

Pizza Roll

Chocolate Clay Pinecones

Pretzel Wreaths

Candy Tree Forest

Little Christmas Mice

CRAFT

Glittering Snow Globes

PIZZA ROLL

This roll delivers the great taste of pizza without the mess. You can also change the meat and cheese filling to suit everyone's taste. Fill them up before starting on the treats to follow!

1 (1-lb.) loaf frozen bread dough, thawed
3 oz. pepperoni (about 25 slices)
1 cup shredded mozzarella cheese (4 oz.)
2 cups favorite pizza or pasta sauce, for dipping

● Heat oven to 325°F. Roll dough out to 12x10-inch rectangle. Top with pepperoni and mozzarella or your favorite meat and cheese combination. Roll dough up jelly-roll fashion; seal seams carefully. Place roll on baking sheet, seam-side down. Cover; let rise about 30 minutes.

● Cut 4 diagonal slashes across top of roll, each about 2 inches long and ¼ inch deep. Bake about 30 minutes or until golden; cool and slice. Heat sauce to serve with roll slices.

12 slices.

Preparation time: 15 minutes.
Ready to serve: 1 hour, 15 minutes.

CHOCOLATE CLAY PINECONES

Your friends will think you picked up their gift under a pine tree. These may look like the real thing, but the combination of chocolate and peanuts makes these cute cones good enough to eat.

12 oz. chocolate chips
½ cup light corn syrup
1 (12-oz.) can cocktail peanuts, halved

● Melt chocolate chips in microwave oven 1 minute; stir to help melt. When melted, stir in corn syrup to blend. Pour mixture onto waxed paper; let harden at least 1 hour or overnight.

● Divide chocolate "clay" into 12 balls. Roll each ball into egg-shaped cone, about 2 inches high and 1 inch across at base. Press end of peanut halves, round-side up, around cones starting at bottom and continuing up to top. Each cone uses 20 to 25 peanut halves.

12 pinecones.

Preparation time: 1 hour, 10 minutes.
Ready to serve: 2 hours, 10 minutes.

PRETZEL WREATHS

The flavor combination of sweet and salty is a dynamic duo. These sweet and salty wreaths woven with a red ribbon also make a great decoration—for as long as they last!

72 miniature pretzel twists
8 oz. vanilla candy coating, melted
6 red ribbon strips, each 12 inches long and ¼ inch wide

● Line 2 baking sheets with waxed paper.

● Using 6 pretzels, form circle on baking sheet, placing side of pretzel with single hole on outside of ring. Remove 1 pretzel; dip inner section into melted candy coating. Replace pretzel; continue with remaining pretzels. To form top wreath layer, dip 6 pretzels into melted coating; place over first circle so coated holes overlap 2 pretzels. Repeat with remaining pretzels and coating to make 6 wreaths.

● Refrigerate until set, about 5 minutes. Weave ribbon through holes around wreaths; tie in a bow.

6 wreaths.

Preparation time: 1 hour.
Ready to serve: 1 hour, 5 minutes.

CANDY TREE FOREST

These candy trees bring out creativity in gift makers as they mix and match candy. Use trees to create a forest, decorate a table or use as place cards ... until, of course, the trees are gobbled up.

 1 **can prepared vanilla frosting**
 6 **drops green food color**
12 **sugar ice cream cones**
 4 **cups variety of small candies, such as gumdrops, Lifesavers®, candy-coated chocolate pieces or chocolate chips**

● Place frosting in medium bowl; stir in food color until mixture is uniform color. Spread frosting generously over outsides of cones. While frosting is soft, press candy all over cones. Let stand until frosting hardens, about 1 hour.

12 trees.

Preparation time: 1 hour.
Ready to serve: 2 hours.

LITTLE CHRISTMAS MICE

"It was the night before Christmas and all through the house not a creature was stirring not even a mouse." Now you can have your own Christmas mice—of chocolate and cherries—and they are very yummy!

20 **Maraschino cherries with stems, drained, dried**
 1 **cup chocolate chips, melted**
20 **chocolate kisses, unwrapped**
40 **almond slices**
   White and red decorator gel

● Holding stem, dip each cherry into melted chocolate; place each on its side on waxed paper, pressing cherry bottom into bottom of chocolate kiss. (The cherry is the body of the mouse, the stem is the tail and the kiss becomes the face.)

● Between kiss and cherry, place 2 almond slices for ears.

● When chocolate has set, about 5 minutes, create eyes by dotting kiss with white gel. Top white gel with tinier dot of red gel.

20 mice.

Preparation time: 45 minutes.
Ready to serve: 50 minutes.

Glittering Snow Globes

These do-it-yourself snow globes are surprisingly easy to make, with a minimum of materials needed. Almost any age child will be successful making one, especially with a little adult assistance. The key to success is the special two-part epoxy glue; no other adhesive will stand up under water (follow package instructions carefully as the epoxy sets up quickly). Any plastic figurine will work, but make sure it fits inside the jar before you begin the project. If the figurine is short, first glue a small stone to the lid, and then the figurine to the stone, to give it added height.

MATERIALS

- **1 pint canning jar per person, complete with lid and ring (before purchasing, check jars to make sure they have at least one side free of embossed letters or designs)**
- **Two-part epoxy glue**
- **1 small bottle glycerin (available, over the counter, at drug stores and pharmacies)**
- **Glitter**
- **Small plastic figurines of your choice**
- **Small rocks, if figurines need bases to stand on**

INSTRUCTIONS

1. Mix two-part epoxy according to label directions.

2. Glue figurine to center of the underside of the lid by placing a little epoxy on each of the figurine's feet or base. Press into place. Epoxy will dry quickly. If using a rock, after gluing the figurine to it, glue the rock to the center of underside of the lid. Let dry for 20 minutes or more.

3. Fill jars with water. Add 2 teaspoons glycerin and 2 teaspoons glitter to water. Water should come to the rim of the jar.

4. Gently place lid with figurine on top of water-filled jar. This will displace excess water so it's best to do this step in a sink.

5. Screw the sealing ring in place. Fasten tightly.

6. Shake jar and watch it snow!

Make-Ahead Holiday Buffet

by Nancy Baggett

Who wants to spend all their time worrying and fretting over the food when there are holidays to be celebrated? There's also a satisfaction in preparing great culinary creations (like these) ahead of time—when you have the time—in warm anticipation of the gathering to come. Serve Cran-Apple Mulled Wine Punch to drink, and delight buffet browsers with Ham and Cheese Puffs, Mediterranean Party Chicken, Roasted Carrots and Onions … and top it all off with Creamy Vanilla Cheesecake with Two-Berry Sauce.

MENU

Cran-Apple Mulled Wine Punch

Ham and Cheese Puffs

Mediterranean Party Chicken

Roasted Carrots and Onions

Creamy Vanilla Cheesecake with Two-Berry Sauce

CRAFT

Miniature Topiary Trees

CRAN-APPLE MULLED WINE PUNCH

This colorful mulled wine punch is a great winter warmer, and fills the air with the scent of fruit and spice.

1½ quarts cran-apple juice
4 or 5 thick orange slices
3 (3- to 4-inch) cinnamon sticks
½ teaspoon whole cloves
¼ to ½ cup sugar, to taste
3 cups (1 bottle) dry red table wine
Thin, seeded orange slices, for garnish
Fresh cranberries, for garnish

● In large nonreactive pot combine juice, thick orange slices, cinnamon sticks, cloves and ¼ cup sugar. Bring just to a boil; reduce heat. Simmer about 15 minutes. Strain juice through fine strainer into plastic or glass storage container. Refrigerate up to 3 days.

● When ready to serve, return juice to large, attractive, nonreactive pot. Add wine; heat to piping hot. Taste; add more sugar, if desired. Float thin orange slices and a few cranberries on top.

9 cups.

Preparation time: 5 minutes.
Ready to serve: 40 minutes.

NOTE Leftover punch can be refrigerated up to several days and reheated.

HAM AND CHEESE PUFFS

Guests may think you ordered these yummy little puff pastry appetizers from a caterer, but since they are made with purchased frozen puff pastry, they are relatively easy to prepare. Ready them up to a month ahead, then simply remove from the freezer, thaw and pop into the oven as needed.

1 (17½-oz.) pkg. frozen puff pastry
   sheets*
4 oz. well-flavored cooked smoked ham,
   trimmed of all fat, diced (about 1 cup)
¼ cup soft (tub-style) cream cheese, at
   room temperature
2 tablespoons unsalted butter, softened
½ teaspoon Dijon mustard
   Generous ¼ teaspoon paprika
1½ cups (6 oz.) grated or shredded
   mozzarella cheese
   About 1 tablespoon milk
¼ cup freshly grated Parmesan cheese

● Thaw pastry; it should be soft enough to work with but still cold and slightly firm. In food processor, process ham, cream cheese, butter, Dijon and paprika until ham is finely ground and spread is completely smooth.

● Unfold and lay out 1 pastry sheet on piece of parchment paper. Spread ham mixture evenly over pastry; sprinkle evenly with mozzarella. Top first pastry sheet with second sheet, pressing firmly all over to seal layers. Brush top layer all over with milk; immediately sprinkle with Parmesan. Slide parchment and pastry onto tray or small baking sheet; loosely cover with waxed paper. Place in freezer until pastry is cold and firm but not hard, 20 to 30 minutes.

● Place parchment with pastry on large cutting board. Using large, sharp knife, cut away any uneven edges so pastry is square; cut crosswise and lengthwise at 1-inch intervals to make 100 (1-inch) squares. (Be sure to cut all the way through dough.) Return parchment and pastry to tray. Cover; freeze until puffs are stiff and frozen, about 30 minutes. Wrap parchment and puffs in waxed paper or foil. Place in large airtight plastic bag; freeze up to 1 month.

● When ready to bake, heat oven to 400°F. Break apart as many frozen puffs from sheet as desired. Arrange puffs about ½ inch apart on parchment- or foil-lined baking sheets. Let stand until completely thawed, about 15 minutes. Bake in upper one-third of oven 7 to 11 minutes or until puffy and golden brown on top. Serve immediately.

TIP *Puff pastry is easier to handle and cut when cool and firm. That's why the recipe calls for returning it to the freezer several times.

100 (1-inch) puffs.

Preparation time: 35 minutes.
Ready to serve: 2 hours.

MEDITERRANEAN PARTY CHICKEN

With this aromatic and savory entree, you have the option of readying the dish several days ahead, an hour ahead or just before you need it. Be sure to use bottled oil-packed sun-dried tomatoes, not dried tomatoes that need to be rehydrated with water.

1⅓ cups canned diced tomatoes
1½ cups bottled roasted red bell peppers, well drained, coarsely chopped
  1 cup pitted Kalamata or other very flavorful black olives
  ¾ cup diced oil-packed sun-dried tomatoes
  ½ cup coarsely chopped green onions, including tender tops
  3 garlic cloves, peeled, minced
    About ⅔ cup extra-virgin olive oil
1½ tablespoons fresh lemon juice
  1 teaspoon dried marjoram
  1 teaspoon dried basil
  ½ teaspoon mild chili powder
  ½ teaspoon salt or to taste
  ¼ teaspoon freshly ground pepper
3⅔ to 4 lb. boneless skinless chicken breast halves (about 8 large), trimmed of fat
  1 lb. rigatoni or ziti pasta, cooked according to pkg. directions
    Fresh parsley or basil sprigs, for garnish (optional)
    Roasted red bell pepper strips, for garnish (optional)

● In very large nonreactive bowl, thoroughly combine diced tomatoes, roasted bell peppers, olives, sun-dried tomatoes, green onions, garlic, ½ cup of the oil, lemon juice, marjoram, basil, chili powder, salt and ground pepper. Cut chicken breast halves lengthwise into thirds. Stir chicken into tomato mixture until incorporated. Cover; refrigerate 1 hour or up to 8 hours.

● Heat oven to 375°F. Divide chicken between 2 flat casseroles large enough to hold chicken without crowding. Bake until chicken pieces are no longer pink in center, 30 to 40 minutes. Turn chicken pieces; baste with pan juices 2 or 3 times during baking. Chicken may be served immediately or covered and held up to 1 hour in warm oven. Or refrigerate and reheat, covered, in low oven. Flavor improves with storage.

● Toss hot cooked pasta with remaining oil. Place pasta on large attractive platter; arrange chicken over pasta. Spoon vegetables and pan juices over chicken. Garnish with parsley and roasted bell pepper strips.

16 cups.

Preparation time: 30 minutes.
Ready to serve: 2 hours, 10 minutes.

ROASTED CARROTS AND ONIONS

This colorful vegetable dish is easy to make ahead and always well received. Initially, the amount of vegetables will seem large, but they cook down a good deal. Also, guests often come back for seconds!

4	**lb. baby carrots**
7 or 8	**large onions, peeled, cut into eighths**
½	**cup extra-virgin olive oil**
1¼	**teaspoons salt or more to taste**
½	**teaspoon dried thyme**
¼	**teaspoon freshly ground pepper or more to taste**
3 to 4	**tablespoons chopped fresh chives or parsley, for garnish**

● Heat oven to 425°F. In extra-large bowl, stir together carrots, onions, oil, salt, thyme and pepper until well blended. Divide vegetables between 2 large roasting or jelly-roll pans. Place pans staggered on 2 racks. Bake, stirring occasionally, 25 minutes. Switch pan positions; continue baking an additional 20 to 30 minutes or until vegetables are cooked through and lightly browned. Taste; add more salt and pepper if desired.

● If serving immediately, transfer to large attractive serving bowl; sprinkle with chives. If making ahead, omit garnish; refrigerate vegetables tightly covered up to 48 hours. Reheat in 350°F oven until piping hot; sprinkle with chives just before serving.

12 servings (10 cups).

Preparation time: 10 minutes.
Ready to serve: 1 hour, 5 minutes.

CREAMY VANILLA CHEESECAKE WITH TWO-BERRY SAUCE

An exceptionally creamy-smooth texture and mellow flavor make this cheesecake more than memorable. A beautiful red raspberry-strawberry sauce becomes the crowning touch.

CRUST
4 oz. vanilla wafers (1½ cups)
¼ cup unsalted butter, chilled, cut into chunks
½ teaspoon vanilla

FILLING
1⅓ cups sugar
2 lb. cream cheese, at room temperature
5 eggs
1 tablespoon very finely grated lemon peel
2 tablespoons Grand Marnier liqueur or orange juice
2½ teaspoons vanilla
½ cup heavy (whipping) cream

SAUCE
2½ tablespoons cornstarch
2 (10-oz.) pkg. frozen raspberries in syrup, thawed
1 tablespoon Grand Marnier liqueur (optional)
1 (10-oz.) pkg. frozen strawberries in syrup

● Heat oven to 350°F. Coat springform pan (9-inch diameter and at least 2¾-inch depth) with nonstick cooking spray. Set out roasting pan large enough to hold springform pan. Center springform pan on 15-inch square of heavy-duty aluminum foil. Carefully pull and smooth excess foil up around pan sides so pan is enclosed in foil all the way around.

● For Crust: In food processor, grind wafers into fine crumbs. Add butter and ½ teaspoon vanilla; process 1 minute or until mixture begins to come together. Press crust evenly and firmly into bottom of springform pan. Bake in upper one-third of oven until lightly browned at edges, 9 to 14 minutes. Cool on wire rack.

● For Filling: Reduce oven temperature to 325°F. In large mixer bowl, beat sugar and cream cheese at low speed 3 to 4 minutes or until completely smooth. Thoroughly scrape down bowl and beater several times to ensure even blending. Add eggs, one at a time, beating to blend. Add lemon peel, 2 tablespoons Grand Marnier and 2½ teaspoons vanilla. Continue beating at low speed until blended and smooth, scraping down bowl often. Slowly add cream; continue beating until batter is blended, scraping down bowl as needed.

● Pour batter (which will be slightly fluid) into springform pan. Shake pan, rapping on counter several times to even surface and release air bubbles. Let stand 10 minutes to allow air bubbles to rise to surface; rap pan on counter again.

● Place springform pan in roasting pan. Transfer to center oven rack. Carefully add enough very hot water to roasting pan to yield depth of at least 1 inch. Bake 15 minutes. Reduce oven temperature to 275°F. Continue baking 1 hour 30 minutes to 1 hour 40 minutes or until cheesecake is set at edges and just barely moves in center when jiggled. Remove cheesecake from water bath; place on wire rack. (Allow pan of water to cool before removing from oven.) Let cheesecake stand to cool and firm 10 minutes. Carefully run paring knife around pan edge to loosen cheesecake from sides. Let cheesecake stand until completely cooled, at least 1½ hours more. Cover; refrigerate until thoroughly chilled, 6 hours or up to 3 days.

● For Sauce: In 2-quart heavy nonreactive saucepan, stir together cornstarch and ¼ cup syrup drained from raspberries. Continue stirring until completely smooth. Drain remaining syrup from raspberries into saucepan, reserving berries. Stir in 1 tablespoon Grand Marnier, if using. Bring mixture to a boil over medium-high heat, stirring constantly. Boil, stirring, just until syrup thickens slightly and becomes clear, 1 to 2 minutes. Gently fold reserved raspberries and strawberries and their syrup into pan. Cook, stirring, 1 minute. Remove from heat; let cool slightly. Refrigerate in nonreactive container until chilled, 2 hours or up to 3 days.

● At serving time, carefully remove springform pan sides. Serve cheesecake directly from pan bottom placed on large serving platter. Present cheesecake with some sauce spooned onto center top. Serve remaining sauce separately, so diners can add it as desired.

12 servings.

Preparation time: 45 minutes. Ready to serve: 10 hours.

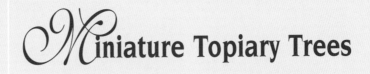

Miniature Topiary Trees

With these miniature topiary trees, it's possible to create a tablescape forest for the holidays. The two larger "trees" can grace a sideboard or mantel, while the smaller ones can serve as props for place cards, one per table setting. You can further decorate the trees with "snow," red berries (real or artificial), miniature garlands, or leave them au naturel. If wrapped carefully in bubble-wrap, these trees can be used from one holiday to the next.

MATERIALS

- **4-inch terra-cotta pots, as many as needed**
- **Plaster of Paris**
- **Coarse sand**
- **¼-inch wooden dowels**
- **Cone- or globe-shaped Styrofoam forms**
- **1 to 2 bags green sphagnum moss**
- **Craft glue**
- **Ribbon of your choice (optional)**

INSTRUCTIONS

1. Mix plaster of Paris in a large bowl according to package directions.

2. Use a large spoon to fill pots with plaster of Paris to about ½ inch below the rim. Immediately push wood dowels into the center of the plaster-filled pots and then sprinkle coarse sand over the wet plaster, gently pressing it into place. Let plaster harden for 30 minutes.

3. Shake off excess sand by turning pots upside down.

4. Cover one side of the Styrofoam form with glue. Press moss into place. Repeat process on the other side of the Styrofoam form. Once completely covered with moss, use both hands to press the moss securely in place.

 *5.* Push moss-covered Styrofoam form onto the top of the wooden dowels.

6. Using scissors, trim moss for a neater appearance.

7. Decorate tree as desired, and tie ribbon into a bow around rim of pot, if you wish.

Christmas Holiday Appetizer Buffet

by Mary Evans

People love appetizers. This fact is key to any successful holiday party. Give your guests a well-chosen selection of snacks and they'll be raving about your party for weeks. Serve all or some of the appetizers to come along with your own personal favorite crowd-pleasers. Make decisions on quantities based on the time of your gathering. If people are coming straight from work in the evening, you'll need to plan on more food than for a mid-afternoon weekend open house. Each recipe here makes a generous amount, and portion sizes allow for at least second helpings of each hors d'oeuvre.

MENU

Black-Eyed Pea Hummus with Pita Crisps

Savory Dried Cherry and Pistachio Biscotti with Blue Cheese Dip

Reuben Crepe Rolls

Pineapple-Topped Ham Pinwheels

Hoisin Chicken Wings

CRAFT

Della Robbia Swag

BLACK-EYED PEA HUMMUS WITH PITA CRISPS

Southerners eat black-eyed peas on the New Year for luck. Here, we've taken these lucky peas and used them instead of the more traditional garbanzos in a Middle-Eastern hummus.

PITA CRISPS
4 (5½- to 6-inch) pita bread rounds

HUMMUS
1 medium garlic clove
1 (15.5-oz.) can black-eyed peas, drained, rinsed
½ teaspoon salt
½ teaspoon ground cumin
Dash cayenne pepper
¼ cup tahini (sesame paste)
¼ cup lemon juice
3 to 4 tablespoons water
1 tablespoon chopped green onion

● Heat oven to 350°F. Cut pitas in half through pocket to form 2 flat circles; cut each circle in 8 wedges. Place wedges on 15x10-inch baking pan; bake 10 to 15 minutes or until pitas are browned and crisp, turning once halfway through.

● Meanwhile, with motor running, drop garlic through feed tube into bowl of food processor. Add black-eyed peas, salt, cumin and cayenne; pulse to coarsely chop. Add tahini and lemon juice; process to thick puree. Add enough water to form soft puree. Stir in green onion. Serve *Hummus* with *Pita Crisps*.

16 servings (1½ cups hummus, with 64 pita crisps).

Preparation time: 20 minutes.
Ready to serve: 20 minutes.

SAVORY DRIED CHERRY AND PISTACHIO BISCOTTI WITH BLUE CHEESE DIP

These savory biscotti make a great appetizer when dunked in creamy blue cheese dip.

BISCOTTI
- 3 eggs
- ¼ cup cornmeal
- 1¾ cups all-purpose flour
- ½ cup shredded Parmesan cheese
- 1 teaspoon baking powder
- ¼ teaspoon salt
- ¼ cup cold butter, cut into pieces
- 1 cup dried cherries
- ¾ cup shelled, salted pistachios

BLUE CHEESE DIP
- 4 oz. blue cheese, such as Maytag blue, crumbled
- ½ cup mayonnaise
- ½ cup buttermilk

● Heat oven to 350°F. Line baking sheet with parchment paper.

● In medium bowl, whisk eggs; whisk in cornmeal. Let rest 10 minutes.

● In food processor, pulse flour, ¼ cup Parmesan, baking powder and salt until combined. Add butter; pulse until butter is cut into fine bits. Add cherries and pistachios; pulse several times to coarsely chop. Add egg mixture; pulse until dough begins to come together. Turn out onto counter; knead briefly to bring together into ball; divide in half. Roll and pat each half into 12x2-inch log. Place on baking sheet. Bake 15 minutes or until set and surface is beginning to crack. Remove; reduce oven temperature to 275°F. Let biscotti rest 10 minutes.

● Cut biscotti into diagonal 1-inch slices. Stagger slices on baking sheet to separate. Return to oven; bake 25 minutes or until just beginning to brown. Rearrange slices close together; sprinkle with remaining ¼ cup Parmesan. Return to oven about 3 minutes or until Parmesan adheres to top. Let cool on wire rack. Store loosely covered to maintain crispness.

● Before serving, blend blue cheese, mayonnaise and buttermilk together. Serve in bowl surrounded by biscotti.

12 servings (1 cup dip, with 24 biscotti).

Preparation time: 30 minutes.
Ready to serve: 1 hour, 30 minutes.

REUBEN CREPE ROLLS

This take-off on wraps uses prepared crepes from the produce section of your supermarket.

1 (5-oz.) pkg. of 10 crepes
½ lb. thinly sliced corned beef
5 tablespoons Thousand Island dressing
1¼ cups well-drained sauerkraut,
  patted dry
1¼ cups (5 oz.) grated Swiss cheese

● Heat oven to 350°F. Stack 2 crepes on top of each other; top with overlapping slices of corned beef. (If crepes are unavailable, use 1 flour tortilla for 2 crepes.) Spread with 1 tablespoon of the dressing. Sprinkle with ¼ cup of the sauerkraut, then with ¼ cup of the grated Swiss cheese.

● Roll into cylinder; place on lightly greased baking sheet. Repeat with remaining ingredients to form 5 cylinders. Bake 5 to 8 minutes or until cheese is just beginning to melt. Remove; let rest 5 minutes to firm.

● Cut on diagonal into 9 pieces each. Serve lukewarm or at room temperature.

15 (3-roll) servings.

Preparation time: 25 minutes.
Ready to serve: 30 minutes.

PINEAPPLE-TOPPED HAM PINWHEELS

Ham, cheese and pineapple combine with puff pastry in this great appetizer.

1 **sheet thawed puff pastry (from 17.3-oz. pkg.)**
2 **tablespoons tomato paste**
¾ **cup finely diced ham**
⅓ **cup grated Swiss or mozzarella cheese**
½ **cup drained pineapple tidbits packed in juice**

● Heat oven to 400°F. Roll puff pastry sheet on lightly floured surface to 12x10-inch rectangle; spread with tomato paste. Sprinkle with ham and then cheese.

● Roll into 12-inch log; trim ends. Cut into 24 (½-inch) slices; place on parchment-lined baking sheets. Bake, 1 sheet at a time, 12 to 14 minutes or until golden brown. Remove; let cool briefly. Top each with 2 pineapple tidbits. Serve warm or at room temperature.

12 (2-pinwheel) servings.

Preparation time: 10 minutes.
Ready to serve: 40 minutes.

HOISIN CHICKEN WINGS

Hoisin sauce is a wonderful, soy-based Chinese product that adds great flavor depth to these mahogany wings. Look for hoisin sauce in the Asian section of your supermarket, or in specialty ethnic markets.

½ **cup hoisin sauce**
¼ **cup ketchup**
¼ **cup soy sauce**
2 **tablespoons sherry**
1 **tablespoon minced garlic**
1 **tablespoon minced fresh ginger**
½ **teaspoon hot pepper sauce**
3 **lb. chicken wings, tips removed, cut in half**

● In large self-sealing bag, combine hoisin sauce, ketchup, soy sauce, sherry, garlic, ginger and hot pepper sauce; squeeze gently to mix ingredients. Add wings; seal and turn to coat. Marinate in refrigerator 1 hour, turning several times.

● Meanwhile, heat oven to 350°F. Line 15x10-inch baking pan with aluminum foil; spray with nonstick cooking spray. Pour wings and marinade into pan; spread to single layer. Bake 30 minutes; turn and bake 45 minutes more, turning every 15 minutes. Serve warm on platter.

15 servings (about 30 pieces).

Preparation time: 20 minutes.
Ready to serve: 2 hours, 35 minutes.

$\mathcal{D}$ella Robbia Swag

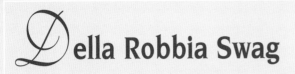

The Della Robbia style dates back to the 15th century when the Florentine sculptor, Luca Della Robbia, found a way to add colorful enamel to his terra-cotta sculpture. Many of his decorative pieces were flat, meant to be permanently attached to a wall, and were surrounded by a terra-cotta "frame" of leaves, fruits and vegetables. The swag shown here is in the Della Robbia style and makes for an unusual and festive holiday decoration, especially when complemented with plenty of pillar candles.

MATERIALS

- Straw swag, long enough to run the length of your table (available at craft supply stores)
- Fresh or artificial magnolia leaves, enough to cover the straw swag
- Florist pins
- An assortment of colorful, small fresh fruits and vegetables, such as grapes, tangerines, radishes, crabapples, persimmons, small eggplants ... whatever is colorful, small and available

INSTRUCTIONS

1. Lay the straw swag out on a flat surface. Cut fresh or artificial magnolia leaves into branchlets of three or four leaves each. Use florist pins to affix leaves to the straw swag until the swag is covered with leaves, all pointing in the same direction, on the top side only.

2. Once leaves are in place, begin adding fruits and vegetables to the swag in a pleasing arrangement of colors and shapes. Use the florist pins to affix the fruits and vegetables to the swag.

3. When complete—and depending on its length— you may need an extra pair of hands to move the swag to its ultimate destination.

Christmas Eve in the Far West

by Cort Sinnes

This is the menu I made for my family's first Christmas Eve dinner the year after I had moved back to California. We wanted to celebrate with foods mostly indigenous to the Far West. It turned out to be an enjoyable meal, not only because everything tasted so good, but because it was so easy to prepare. In reminiscing, I realized that just about all the featured foods—from artichokes to crab to persimmon sorbet—were served pretty much just as nature had created them. It was yet another reminder that by starting with the best possible ingredients, the cook need not go to great effort to present a memorable meal. We served chilled Champagne throughout the meal, but any dry white wine will do nicely.

MENU

Cream of Leek, Potato and Celery Soup

Meringues with Fresh Persimmon Sorbet

Fresh Dungeness Crab with Steamed Artichokes and Dijonnaise Sauce

CRAFT

Evergreen Citrus Wreath

CREAM OF LEEK, POTATO AND CELERY SOUP

Over the years this soup has become the traditional "starter" for our Christmas Eve celebration, primarily because my daughter is crazy about it. The addition of celery to the more common leek and potato soup elevates its flavor. Depending on the formality of your dinner, it can be served in warm bowls at the table, or in mugs, before your guests have been seated, as a soul-warming signal that dinner is about to be served.

3 **tablespoons butter**
6 **leeks, white part only, cleaned thoroughly, thinly sliced**
5 **large ribs celery, thinly sliced**
5 **cups reduced-sodium chicken or vegetable broth, plus more if needed**
2 **large baking potatoes, peeled, thinly sliced**
1 **cup milk, plus more if needed**
   Salt to taste
¼ **teaspoon ground white pepper**
   Finely chopped fresh parsley, for garnish

● In large soup pot, melt butter over medium heat. Add leeks and celery; sauté, stirring frequently, until softened, 8 to 10 minutes. Add broth; bring to a boil. Stir in potatoes; return to a boil, partially covered. Reduce heat to medium. Cook until potatoes are soft and begin to fall apart, stirring occasionally to keep potatoes from sticking to bottom of pan, 10 to 15 minutes. Once cooked, remove pot from heat to cool.

● With slotted spoon, place vegetables in blender or food processor; in small batches, puree until smooth, adding liquid as needed. Return puree to pot over medium heat. Add milk, salt and white pepper; bring just to a boil. Add additional broth or milk until soup is desired consistency. Taste; adjust seasoning if needed. Serve in warm soup bowls or mugs, garnished with parsley.

13 cups.

Preparation time: 50 minutes.
Ready to serve: 1 hour, 15 minutes.

MERINGUES WITH FRESH PERSIMMON SORBET

For all its simplicity, this is a spectacular dessert and, somewhat surprisingly, relatively low-fat. From Halloween through the first part of December, bright orange persimmons hang from bare trees looking for all the world like decorated Christmas trees. The trick is to buy or pick persimmons ahead of time, let them ripen at room temperature until fully soft and ripe, and then slip them in the freezer until you're ready to use them.

4	**egg whites**
¾	**cup sugar**
½	**teaspoon vanilla**
¼	**teaspoon vinegar**
8	**fully ripe persimmons, peeled, cored, quartered, frozen**
1	**bag frozen raspberries, thawed**
	Good-quality vanilla ice cream
½	**cup chopped pistachios**

● To prepare meringues: Heat oven to 250°F. Line baking sheet with parchment paper; draw 8 (4-inch) circles on parchment. In large bowl, beat egg whites with electric mixer at medium speed until soft peaks form. Add sugar, 1 tablespoon at a time, beating at high speed until stiff glossy peaks form. Fold in vanilla and vinegar. Spoon meringue onto circles on baking sheet, building up edges to form 1-inch-tall sides. Bake meringues 1 hour. Do not open oven while meringues are baking. After 1 hour, turn oven off. Leave meringues in oven with door closed 2 hours.

● To prepare sorbet: Remove persimmon quarters from freezer; let thaw 5 to 10 minutes. In food processor, pulse persimmons until pureed. Place in bowl; cover with plastic wrap. Return to freezer until needed.

● To prepare sauce: Pour thawed raspberries into large sieve. Using back of large spoon, press raspberries through sieve, catching juice in small bowl. Reserve juice in refrigerator until needed.

● To assemble: Place individual meringues on dessert plates. Remove persimmon sorbet from freezer; fluff lightly with fork. Top meringues with 1 scoop ice cream and 1 scoop sorbet. Drizzle sauce over top; sprinkle with pistachios.

8 filled meringues.

Preparation time: 1 hour.
Ready to serve: 3 hours, 30 minutes.

FRESH DUNGENESS CRAB WITH STEAMED ARTICHOKES AND DIJONNAISE SAUCE

Nothing like a main course that demands no preparation from the cook! Dungeness crab is a true gourmet delight just the way it comes from the sea. Luckily, speedy distribution has made it available nationwide, but only in months with an "r" in them. Luckily, December has that all-important "r."

● Count on 1 crab per person. Have crabs cleaned and cracked at the store. Cook to doneness. Store in refrigerator until just before serving. Mound cooked crabs on large platter filled with layer of ice. Provide empty bowls for discarded shells, and plenty of lemon wedges, mayonnaise or *Dijonnaise Sauce* (recipe follows). If you can find them, small crab forks make removing the delicious meat an easy task. Eating cracked crab is a "hands-on" experience, more than a little messy, so providing hot, moist washcloths (you can heat moist washcloths in the microwave) is a nice touch once everyone has finished eating.

Steamed Artichokes

● Count on 1 large artichoke per person. In Europe, it's not unusual for artichokes to be served on their sides (or upside down) as the stem is almost as flavorful as the artichoke heart. If you decide to serve them this way, simply trim ¼ inch or so from stem. If you want to serve artichokes upright, cut off entire stem—in a straight line—so artichokes stand squarely on their base. With large, very sharp knife, cut approximately ½ inch straight across tops of artichokes. Using scissors, cut tips (which have sharp thorns) from leaves. To prevent cut ends from turning dark, place trimmed artichokes in pan of cold water, acidulated with fresh lemon juice.

● Steam artichokes by placing upside down on steaming basket over 1 to 2 inches boiling water. Cook, covered, over medium heat until tender, about 45 minutes for large artichokes. Artichokes are tender when an individual leaf pulls easily from base. Serve with mayonnaise, lemon juice or *Dijonnaise Sauce* (recipe follows).

DIJONNAISE SAUCE

This easy-to-make sauce is a flavorful step up from plain mayonnaise, and you can serve it with both the artichokes and the cracked crab.

1 cup good-quality mayonnaise
1½ tablespoons Dijon mustard
Juice of 1 lemon
Dash hot pepper sauce

● In small bowl, mix together mayonnaise, Dijon, lemon juice and hot pepper sauce. Store, covered, in refrigerator until ready to serve.

1 cup.

Preparation time: 5 minutes.
Ready to serve: 5 minutes.

vergreen Citrus Wreath

Unless you reside in a region of extremely mild winters, it may come as a surprise that December is the month when most of our prized citrus fruits ripen to perfection. Given their glowing colors, they make a perfect— if unusual—option for natural holiday ornaments. Shown here is a traditional evergreen wreath decorated with tangerines, lemons and limes instead of the more typical holly berries. A real eye-catcher in any part of the country, this wreath is complemented by pillar candles in their own citrus colors.

MATERIALS

- **Round wreath form, either straw or Styrofoam**
- **Fresh evergreen boughs**
- **Selection of fresh citrus—limes, tangerines and lemons—enough to circle the wreath**
- **Florist pins**
- **Florist wire**
- **Pillar candles, in three different heights**

INSTRUCTIONS

1. Cut evergreen branches into approximately 7-inch lengths. Bundle 3 or 4 of the short branches together. Attach the bundles of branches to the wreath form using either florist wire or florist pins (note that you may find the pins easier to use than the wire).

2. Continue adding bundles of branches to the wreath, all pointing in the same direction and overlapping slightly, until wreath is completely covered on one side only.

3. Cut florist wire into 16-inch lengths and form into a hook on one end. Thread the hook end through the citrus on the side that will be next to the wreath. Bend the remaining wire around the wreath to hold the citrus firmly in place.

4. Place the wreath on the table and position pillar candles in the center, making sure no open flame will come near the wreath's foliage.

INDEX